About the Author:

Colin Murray Turbayne is Professor Emeritus of Philosophy at the University of Rochester. In this book, the author of the acclaimed *The Myth of Metaphor* continues his interest in metaphor and the philosophy of the mind.

Metaphors for the Mind

Metaphors For the Mind:

The Creative Mind and Its Origins

Colin Murray Turbayne

University of South Carolina Press

Copyright © 1991 University of South Carolina

Published in Columbia, South Carolina, by the
University of South Carolina Press

Manufactured in the United States of America

Library of Congress Cataloging-in-Publication Data

Turbayne, Colin Murray.
   Metaphors for the mind : the creative mind and its origins / Colin
Murray Turbayne.
     p.   cm.
   Includes bibliographical references and index.
   ISBN 0-87249-699-6
   1. Philosophy of mind—History. 2. Metaphor—History.   I. Title.
BD418.3.T87 1990
128'.2—dc20   90-38182
                                                                         CIP

For Ailsa

*who corrects my proofs
as well as my stories*

Having now my method by the end,
Still as I pulled it came

John Bunyan,
Pilgrim's Progress

Contents

List of Figures	xii
Preface	xiii
Introduction	1
1 Exploding the Subject-Predicate Myth: **The Way We See the World**	7
Plato's Myth	8
The Subject-Predicate Myth	9
Hume's Skepticism	11
Ramsey's Skepticism	13
The Two Models	15
Conclusion: A Weakness in Subject-Predicate Theories of Mind	21
2 Exposing the Root Metaphor: **Plato's Androgynous Cosmos**	22
Plato's Fantastic Appendix	23
The Nature of the *Timaeus*	23
The Craftsman Model	27
The Procreation Model	28
Procreation as a Model for the Cosmos	32
Unity of the *Timaeus*	39
Conclusion: Procreation as a Model for the Mind	41
3 Using the Metaphor: **Aristotle's Androgynous Mind**	42
Passive and Active Minds	42
Problems and Solutions	43
The Metaphorical Way	44
Aristotle's Procreation Model	45

	Nutrition	47
	Perception	48
	Imagination and Willing	56
	Passive and Active Minds Revisited	58
	Passive Mind	58
	Active Mind	60
	The Trinity	63
	Conclusion: The End of the Search for Origins	64
4	**Resuscitating the Metaphor I:** **Berkeley's Understanding and Will**	67
	Problems	68
	Solutions	69
	"Act" and Object	71
	Plato's Receptacle and Berkeley's Mind	74
	Aristotle's Subject and Berkeley's Mind	76
	Conclusion: Berkeley's Androgynous Mind	80
5	**Resuscitating the Metaphor II:** **Kant's Passive and Active Mind**	82
	The Passive Sensibility and the Active Understanding	83
	Problems	83
	Faculties in Plato and Aristotle	84
	Kant's Copernican Revolution	85
	"Aristarchus" and "Copernicus"	89
	Passive and Active Minds	92
	Conclusion: Kant's Mind-Centered Universe	93

Contents   xi

**6 Finding an Auxiliary Model:
   The Mind as Reader and Writer**   95

    The Problem   96

    The Traditional Doctrine:
   The Camera Model   97

    A Rival Hypothesis:
   To See is to Read   99

    Dropping the Copy Theory:
   The Two Languages   100

    Learning to Read   103

    Word Magic   106

    Writing in Ordinary and Visual Language   108

    Conclusion: 116
       How We Make Our Worlds

Notes   119

Name Index   129

Subject Index   131

Figures

2.1	Man as a micropolis	25
2.2	Man as a microcosm	26
2.3	The Craftsman Model	28
2.4	The combination of Necessity and Intelligence	29
2.5	The Procreation Model	29
2.6	The Procreation Model	31
2.7	The birth of the cosmos	33
2.8	The generative power in the world: *Hermes*	35
2.9	The chromosomes of the cosmos	38
3.1	Aristotle's Procreation Model	46
3.2	Aristotle's androgynous plant	48
3.3	The son of Diares	50
3.4	Plato's twins	52
3.5	Aristotle's trinity	63
6.1	Illusion	96
6.2	The camera	97
6.3	Photographic distortion	98
6.4	*Linear Construction*	99
6.5	The two languages	101
6.6	The owl and the crocodile, hieroglyph	102
6.7	The squares	107
6.8	The duck-rabbit	107
6.9	*Thoth*, Egyptian god of writing	108
6.10	*The Seated Scribe*	109
6.11	*Reclining Nude*	111
6.12	*Head of a Woman*	114
6.13	*Winged Victory of Samothrace*	115
6.14	Second lesson in reading	117
6.15	Sentence from the Book of Nature	118

Preface

In this book I use the "metaphorical way" to expose a fundamental imbalance in our traditional views of the mind and to try to restore the balance that has been lost.

The metaphorical way offers a novel approach to the solution of certain problems in philosophy and its history. It enables me to bring to the surface the root metaphors submerged in our thinking about the mind and to suggest an alternative view.

Using this method I try to expose and to delineate one of the most powerful conceptual devices in the history of the mind, one that has been hidden or neglected almost from the time of its conception in Plato's work. This is the Procreation Model. Although its power and fecundity were manifested in the fragments of the pre-Socratics and embedded in the subconscious of the Western world before the Greeks, Plato was the first to apply this device in a systematic way, not to the structure and operations of the mind but to those of the cosmos. It was Plato's student, Aristotle, I argue, who was the first to use it to make a theory of mind.

From that time it has exerted enormous underground influence on subsequent conceptions of mind. I show this influence in the works of important modern thinkers such as Berkeley and Kant. The model enables me to restore features in our traditional conceptions so that the female and the male hemispheres of the mind work as partners. Finally, in order to restore further the balance that has been lost I present an auxiliary model of mind, that of Reader and Writer, in which the traditional passivity of the female hemisphere gives way to active receptivity.

Why has the Procreation Model been neglected or covered up? The answer might lie in the vehicle of the metaphor itself, namely, sex and procreation. Plato and Aristotle were ready to discuss these topics—the former in his fantastic appendix to *Timaeus* and the latter in his masterpiece, *Generation of Animals*—but until very recently we in the Western world, perhaps owing to religious bias, have tended to elevate the mind at the expense of the body and to smother discussion of sex and procreation.

The chapters in the book are based upon the following articles:

"The Subject-Predicate Myth," *Studies in the Twentieth Century,* I, no. 1 (Spring 1968), pp. 7–20.

"Visual Language from the Verbal Model," *Journal of Typographic Research,* later called *Visible Language* III, no. 4 (Oct. 1969), pp. 345–70.

Italian translation: Estratto dalla Rivista, *Luce e Immagini* 586, xxiv, n. 5 (Settembre-Ottobre 1970), pp. 137–50, 591; xxiv, n. 6 (Novembre-Decembre, 1970), pp. 180–85.

"Plato's Fantastic Appendix: The Procreation Model of the Timaeus," *Paideia: Special Plato Issue* (1976), pp. 125–40. Dutch translation as Introduction to *Timaios* in *Platoon Verzameld Werk* (Amsterdam: De Driehoek, 1986) IV, pp. 11–45.

"Aristotle's Androgynous Mind," *Paideia: Special Aristotle Issue,* 1 (1979), pp. 30–49.

"Kant's Passive and Active Mind: The Kant, Plato, Aristotle Connection," a paper delivered at a Kant Conference in honor of Lewis White Beck on the occasion of his retirement, at the University of Rochester, on April 11, 1979.

"Lending a Hand to Philonous: The Berkeley, Plato, Aristotle Connection," in Colin M. Turbayne, ed., *Berkeley, Critical and Interpretive Essays* (Minneapolis: University of Minnesota Press, 1982), pp. 295–310.

There are many people I wish to thank for helping me throughout this work. Among them are: Morse Peckham for his support for my ideas on metaphor; George C. Simmons, Editor of *Paideia,* for his generous encouragement and advice in the writing of the articles, "Plato's Fantastic Appendix" and "Aristotle's Androgynous Mind"; Stephanie Frontz of Rush Rhees Art Library, University of Rochester, for locating the source of the works of art; my students over the years who helped with their enthusiasm for philosophy and eagerness to adventure with me into that strange world of the mind; for the readers of the manuscript selected by the Press, for their perspicacious criticisms and suggestions; Paul Hammer of Colgate Rochester Divinity School for his valued advice on *pneuma* in the *New Testament*; Lynne McCoy for her work in typing the original version; Armanda Balduzzi for providing one of the indispensable props for completing the manuscript; my son Ronald for his penetrating questions on the manuscript, which enabled me to eradicate some of the weaknesses in the book; my son John for his technical suggestions and advice on the title; and finally, my helpmate, Ailsa, who has worked indefatigably but with lightness of spirit, helping me with the heavy task of getting this book ready for publication, who has listened to my ideas over the years, and who has even volunteered to shoulder some of the responsibility for them except for the mistaken ones.

University of Rochester C.M.T.
September 1989

Metaphors for the Mind

Introduction

The history of the mind, called by Kant "the enchanted island," records so many different attempts to explore, chart, and describe its geography that one wonders whether all explorers have been focused on the same island.

In the following pages I try to reduce the many accounts to a few, to isolate prominent themes running through the history, and to reveal the common origins of those themes. I hope also to rediscover some important parts of the island for which the charts have been destroyed or distorted.

One chart, however has been so much redrawn and so long referred to that the majority of us in this century still accept something like it almost instinctively. This is the view, hailing from a time much before Descartes, that the mind is a thing or a substance, having properties or attributes, and thus is almost a mirror image in the mental realm of the outside world as one consisting of material substances with material attributes. On the face of it, this view is much the same as the one implicit in Socrates' reply to Crito's question, "How shall we bury you, Socrates?": "Any way you like, provided you can catch me and prevent me from escaping you. . . . So be of good cheer and say that you are burying my body, and do that in any fashion you please and seems to you to conform best to custom."

Since the seventeenth century when Descartes established it, this chart or theory has been on the defensive. In the same century Hobbes attacked it, not because of the presence of substance in it but because that substance was mental instead of material. In the next century Hume attacked it because he was unable to find any substance at all. More recently Gilbert Ryle has claimed that the theory makes one giant "category mistake"; that is, it represents the facts of mental life as if they were physical facts when actually they are mental ones. Although it has been under siege for the last three centuries, it remains, I believe, as secure as ever and deserves Ryle's title, "the official theory."[1]

In spite of its appeal and utility, the substance-attribute theory has always seemed to me to have something radically wrong with it. My reasons for rejecting the doctrine are different from those just given. For a start, it seems to me not to fit with some fundamental beliefs that we have about ourselves. Once we think of our minds as substances with attributes, even though these attributes be active ones, we cannot avoid thinking of ourselves as passive beings. This is because no matter how independent, solid, substantial, and supportive substances are, they cannot help but suggest "standing under" or supporting in the way that pillars support a building, carrying no suggestion of power or activity. At the same time, we sense and believe that we are powerful, active, creative beings. Thus the weakness at the basis of the official theory is that it fails to accommodate our stubbornly held beliefs about ourselves. To the objection that power, activity, and creativity are still present but are attributes of the mind as substance, my reply is that attributes suggest incompleteness and dependency, which cannot exist unless supported by mind as substance, and this suggests passivity once more.

Influenced perhaps by a long line of philosophers, most of us accept the official theory in one hemisphere of our minds (the verbal, analytical, rational one) but through our feelings, reject it in the other hemisphere (the nonverbal, holistic, intuitive one). This contradiction may also be the manifestation of a deep confusion in us, associated with much of the intellectual unbalance in the world; the deficiencies noted by Hobbes, Hume, Ryle, and a host of others (including myself) may be symptoms of a deeper malady.

From the time of Freud, many psychotherapists have accepted the view that the infant, metaphorically speaking, is parent of the adult. If I as a therapist desire to diagnose an adult's ailment before trying to prescribe a cure, I spend no time in prescribing drugs to suppress the symptoms but trace these symptoms to their source in the patient's infancy so that I can prescribe a different remedy. Perhaps we shall find that awareness itself, say of being left alone in a dark room as an infant, will be sufficient therapy for an adult's claustrophobia. The aim of my psychotherapy, as I suspect it is of all such practice, is to bring the conscious mind of the patient into balance and harmony with the deepest intuitions and feelings.

Let me treat our present perplexity about the mind in an analogous way, that is, as an etiology of a modern malady. Accepting that something is radically wrong with the official doctrine, I shall spend no time trying to repair the logic of the substance-attribute theory at this stage but try instead to trace it to its source in the beginnings of our culture so that we can become aware of the mistake. Is there, then, an error made by a great sort-crosser (or metaphor maker) of the past who, having tried to allocate the facts in a new way, then left his re-allocation as a legacy of dubious value to posterity? Could it be that this inventor took a wrong turning, or was that turning taken by his followers?

Introduction

To understand the predicament of the present age I have found it increasingly important to study the great thinkers of the past, especially the Greeks, on whom our Western culture is based. In those cultures our assumptions, so fundamental that we do not know we make them, were not taken for granted. Accordingly, I begin by studying some of the most influential ideas in our history, those found in the writings of Plato and Aristotle. Fortunately, one of these thinkers is, I believe, the master of metaphor in western philosophy.

In the search for origins I make use of what I call "the metaphorical way." This is not an unusual approach. Poets and students of literature have always been aware that metaphor is at the heart of literary matters although in philosophy students have been slower to realize the importance of metaphor. In the sciences it has been traditional to draw a sharp distinction between bona fide science and scientific mythology. Scientists have been the last to accept the apparently implausible view that metaphor, closely associated as it is with such unscientific modes of thought as poetic fancy and imagination, plays a stellar role in the construction of great scientific theories. At present, however, there is an upsurge of interest in metaphor, together with an awareness that metaphor is not confined to poetry but pervades all disciplines.

By metaphor I mean the representation of the facts as if they belonged to one sort or category when they actually belong to another.[2] The extended metaphor provides the key to my search for the origins of mind as well as a connecting link between science and philosophy. In using it, the author specifies various features of his metaphor that make a system. This system constitutes, in the appropriate idioms, an extended metaphor. In the idioms appropriate to scientific theories, it constitutes a model. Plato's extended metaphors are sustained not just through a page or two but, like Bunyan's *Pilgrim's Progress,* throughout a whole book. An effective metaphor, invented by a genius and extended to make an entire theory, tends to pass into another stage: from conscious metaphor into unconscious myth, from make-believe into belief. The passage is hastened if the machinery of comparison is hidden or half-hidden by the inventor or ignored by his followers, and the metaphor goes underground. After all this time, some of Plato's metaphors are not obvious to most of us. Perhaps we never thought it worth our while to look for them because we considered them just literary or stylistic devices.

The two stages in the life of a metaphor manifest two remarkable powers of the human mind. The first power is the ability to devise conceptual structures and project them on reality. The second is the tendency to become oblivious to the fictitious character of these conceptual structures. If one really is to understand what a philosopher such as Plato, Aristotle, Newton, or Einstein says, one must detect the fundamental idea behind the philosophy. But this may have appeared so obvious to the philosopher that he has not bothered to disclose it or may even be unaware of it. Such a guiding idea, deeply rooted in a philosopher's thought and from which many of his other ideas derive or grow, I call a "root metaphor."

In this search for origins a main problem has been bringing to the surface these extended metaphors submerged or partially submerged in the writings of influential metaphysicians of the past. This is a problem requiring the skill of a detective. The clues are found in the finished vocabulary of the theory as it has come down to us. All this is a problem of analysis whose solution is found when, having become aware of the metaphors involved, we attempt to see how the metaphysicians have used them, either with awareness or like sleepwalkers. But there is another problem—one of synthesis or creativity. Having brought to the surface the submerged metaphors, need we use the same ones? If we are aware, we can stop and think. We can choose our metaphors. We are no longer duped citizens of the city-state of Oz; we are the Wizard of Oz himself. In our search for the best possible metaphors we can either use the old ones or, if these are worn out by time or overuse, invent new ones. But, perhaps most importantly, I find that traces of the former live metaphor remain and are giveaways of the images or guiding ideas of the philosopher's thought.

In the first chapter I attempt to expose the nature of two closely related conceptions in Western thought on which the substance view of the mind depends. I contend that the substance-attribute dichotomy in the world and its parallel subject-predicate distinction in language, far from existing in the structure of the world or as innate ideas, are conceptual tools devised to satisfy human interests and needs. Similar to Plato's Myth of the Earth-Born, which reinforces a class structure similar to ours, they are models, used unwittingly to set up, among other theories, a traditional theory of mind.

In the second chapter I find the bases of our substance-attribute views about the mind. Astonishingly, I discover them of all places in Plato's *Timaeus*, a book purporting to be on cosmogony and cosmology and having enormous influence on the rise of modern science. Readers may wonder why I devote so many pages to this mysterious work that has bewildered commentators from Plato's time to ours. I have done so because I believe that clues, not only to the real nature of the *Timaeus*,

Introduction

but also to the origins of modern theories of mind, are to be found in Plato's "fantastic" appendix, which has been dismissed as a playful diversion. It turns out that the *Timaeus* is not primarily a book on cosmogony or cosmology but on the nature of man and woman. It turns out also that this appendix leads directly to the discovery of Plato's Procreation Model from which I believe is developed the substance-attribute dichotomy, as well as modern theories of mind. Finally this chapter shows how extended metaphors can be used to analyze the thought of a philosopher, as well as how to develop theories.

Plato's Procreation Model, which he used to set up his theory of the cosmos, is brought down to earth, so to speak, in the third chapter. Here I show how Aristotle uses it to model the human soul and mind. The model is not overt but is, I believe, revealed to us between the lines by Aristotle the biologist, who was about to complete his masterpiece, *Generation of Animals,* itself perhaps a development from Plato's appendix. On careful scrutiny, this model enables one to understand Aristotle's psychology, which I outline here with special attention to rescuing the active mind from the scrap heap, where it has been relegated by many moderns. This model also supports the claim that, with the help of Aristotle's other writings, here we find the embryo of the substance-attribute and substance-inherence theories of mind. The reader will notice reference to androgyny in the titles of these two chapters, indicating the direction I take to suggest a remedy for the intellectual unbalance associated with the substance-attribute view of the mind.

Although the Procreation Model goes underground for the next two thousand years, its influence persists. This is seen in chapters four and five, in the contributions of two philosophers of the Enlightenment, Berkeley and Kant. Repeated in their writings are the notions of passive and active minds, of faculty psychology, of joint product, of the power of the active mind, and of the given in perception. Berkeley elevates Aristotle's "willing" into a faculty called the Will. Perhaps directly influenced by Aristotle, he comes right out and says that this is the "mind-active," a creator that can make and unmake ideas. But Berkeley is more interested in developing his account of the passive mind (the Understanding) and the notion of "in the mind," which echoes Plato's Receptacle. In Kant, on the other hand, we find modern philosophy's best example of the development of the notion of the creative mind as well as the notion of a joint product of the active and passive mind. On the question of substance and attribute, however, although we find Berkeley rejecting it, Kant appears to sustain it.

In the final chapter, I depart from the use of the Procreation Model in order to set up a helpful auxiliary, the model of the mind as Reader and Writer. This model has the same fundamental structure, that is, the two hemispheres of the mind, but one is transformed from passivity into receptivity; it shows the mind working with symbols in learning to operate with two languages; it shows the creative mind at work in the way we make our worlds; and it does all this without resorting to the substance-attribute concept.

On this voyage to the enchanted island of the mind, the reader can travel in several ways. If the voyager is persuaded to read further in this book, then I suggest a slow cruise from New York to the Greek Islands and return, with time to stop and contemplate the sights; the book can then be read from beginning to end. If only a quick air trip is possible with stop-overs in Dublin and Königsburg, the traveler can read the beginning and the conclusion of each chapter and think of the rest of the book as a series of footnotes. Perhaps, however, it is possible only to make a quick trip by Concorde, in which case the reader can pause only over the table of contents.

CHAPTER 1

Exploding The Subject-Predicate Myth:
The Way We See The World

The distinction between sensible qualities and the substance to which they belong, and between thought and the mind that thinks, is not the invention of philosophers; it is found in the structure of all languages and, therefore, must be common to all men who speak with understanding.

Thomas Reid

Two parallel and closely related ideas are deeply entrenched in our conceptual scheme. One concerns the structure of the world, including the structure of the human mind, the other the structure of language. According to the first, the objects of the world are of two sorts: specifically, substances and their attributes, or particulars and universals. So fundamental is this division that one could claim with considerable justification that we start to think by learning to recognize the same universal in many particulars and many universals in the same particular. According to the second conception, the sentences of our language consist of two parts: specifically, subjects and their predicates. So elementary is this distinction that our first lessons in analysis and composition are devoted to showing how we ascribe the same predicate to different subjects and different predicates to the same subject.

My purpose is to reveal the nature of these fundamental conceptions. I wish to show that the substance-attribute dichotomy and the subject-predicate distinction form two remarkable conceptual devices probably invented by great sort-crossers of the past for the purpose of sorting facts expeditiously. First, I shall illustrate the character of my hypothesis from Plato's account of the Myth of the Earth-Born, showing how deeply entrenched are these conceptions in our Western tradition. Next, I shall explore three stages of skepticism with regard to the conceptions, ending with a skepticism similar to Plato's in regard to his own invention. Finally, I shall try to reveal a difficulty in theories of mind based upon these distinctions.

PLATO'S MYTH

In Book III of the *Republic* Plato invents a myth (*mythos*), a convenient fiction (*pseudos*), the Myth of the Earth-Born. By means of this artificial contrivance (*mechane*) the whole community is to be persuaded to believe in the class structure. Having presented the myth, Plato concludes: "Such is the myth. How are we going to get them to believe it? The generation to whom it is first told cannot possibly believe it, but the next may, and the generations after, and thus the public good may be served. . . . So we shall leave the success of our myth to the care of popular tradition."

Let us suppose that popular tradition (*pheme*) has taken good care of Plato's myth and that it is a success; in which case, in generations after, it has ceased to be a convenient fiction and now is accepted as true. The great majority of us now firmly believe that the distinction between the classes is ultimate and that we are all actually autochthonous, some of us having gold in our makeup, others silver, and so on. These beliefs are entrenched in our conceptual scheme alongside such others as that we all possess immaterial souls. The two conceptions, moreover, are now confused. This confusion is manifested in the fusion of the two vocabularies. The two upper classes are often referred to as "the golden" and "the silver" classes, while the lower class is referred to as "the brass and the iron" class.

A small minority, however, is distrustful of the reality of these distinctions. One skeptic investigates the class structure itself. Finding no external evidence for the belief in the distinction between the classes, he pronounces it false and claims that we are all lower class.

Another skeptic, more sophisticated than the first, turns his attention to the basis of the class structure. He investigates the chemical composition of the members. He finds no essential distinction between the classes with respect to the presence of precious and cheap metals in their makeup. He claims that this throws doubt upon the whole basis of the distinction between the upper and the lower classes, and, as deduced from that between the precious and cheap metals in the make-up of the members. Accordingly, he drops the class distinction.

A third skeptic adopts a point of view similar to that of Plato. For him the story of the Earth-Born is a myth. That is to say, it is neither true nor false but merely an artificial contrivance or instrument analogous to a theatrical machine hidden behind the scenes, designed to make the gods appear. His thesis is perhaps more revolutionary than Plato's, for he claims that the class system also is a myth. He tells us that these

The Way We See the World

two conceptions are appropriately treated as of the same order as explanatory devices or models used in science, one of which functions as an auxiliary of the other. He brings to the surface the parallels between the two and separates the metal vocabulary from the political vocabulary. Although he concedes their enormous utility, he suggests their replacement by alternative devices.

THE SUBJECT-PREDICATE MYTH

The substance-attribute and subject-predicate conceptions have long since reached the stage that Plato predicted for the Myth of the Earth-Born. An eighteenth-century champion of common sense, Thomas Reid, claimed that they were not products of "invention" but were part of "reality" and impervious to "skeptical" argument: "The distinction between sensible qualities and the substance to which they belong, and between thought and the mind that thinks, is not the invention of philosophers; it is found in the structure of all languages and therefore must be common to all men who speak with understanding. And I believe no man, however skeptical he may be in speculation, can talk on the common affairs of life for half an hour without saying things that imply his belief in the reality of these distinctions."[1] One can readily see how Reid and others can envisage such a close connection between the structure of language and the structure of the world. Certainly all the Indo-European languages lend themselves to the subject-predicate analysis. In 1911 Bertrand Russell said of the particular-universal distinction, "My own opinion is that the dualism is ultimate," and of the subject-predicate distinction that "predication is an ultimate relation."[2] A more recent detender is P. F. Strawson. His defense consists in showing that the parallel depends upon "the crucial idea of completeness" present in subjects and expressions introducing particulars into discourse and absent in predicates and expressions introducing universals. This argument is embedded in an overall argument for commonsense beliefs akin to those of Thomas Reid, or what Strawson calls "the conceptual scheme with which we operate." Since "a central place among particulars must be accorded to material bodies and persons," and since "particulars hold a central place among logical subjects . . . i.e., among things in general," Strawson argues, "persons and the material bodies are what primarily exist." He thus gives a "rational account" of our "stubbornly held" beliefs, things that "we believe on instinct."[3]

Traditionally, the parallel between the two distinctions has not been directly discussed. Instead, "the reality of these distinctions," like that of a law of thought, has been taken for granted. Metaphysicians in general have built their systems of the nature of man and the physical world within this conceptual framework without bothering to examine the frame. As an example I choose a central argument of Descartes, the most influential of modern philosophers. Descartes did not try to alter our conceptions. On the contrary, he assumed the reality of the substance-attribute distinction and used it to "demonstrate" the existence of mental substance and material substance. This is seen in the argument for his famous "cogito ergo sum," not in *Meditation* II but in the *Third Set of Objections,* where he is pressed by Hobbes. He first accepts the as yet uninterpreted substance-attribute axiom, "No activity, no attribute can exist without a substance in which to exist."[4] Then, admitting that "we do not apprehend the substance itself immediately through itself, but by means only of the fact that it is the subject of certain activities," and interpreting thought as an activity or attribute, he is able to conclude: "It is certain that no thought can exist apart from a thing that thinks." Following the requirement merely of custom, for the time being he calls the substance in which the attribute thought exists "the mind" or "the self." Whether this substance is the same as or distinct from that other substance, namely, the body, he leaves "wholly undetermined until *Meditation* VI." This argument, of course, leaves Descartes' "cogito ergo sum" unproved, but it does exhibit the nature of his apparatus. Appropriately, in the original version of *Meditation* II, Descartes wrote only "cogitatio est; haec sola a me divelli nequit. Ergo sum," that is, "Thinking exists; this alone cannot be divested from me. Therefore I exist." Accordingly, his famous argument "Cogito ergo sum" is elliptical for "Cogitatio est, ergo res cogitans est," or, "Thinking exists; therefore thinking substance exists," which, in turn, abbreviates the argument just presented. His ulterior conclusion is that the human mind or soul is a "pure substance." That is, "even if all its accidents change . . . nevertheless it still remains the same soul. . . From this it follows that the mind is immortal by its very nature."

One would expect to find, after all this time, some fusion of the subject-predicate and substance-attribute conceptions, and this should be manifested in a partial fusion of the two vocabularies. This expectation is confirmed in the writings of many subscribers to the traditional doctrine who use interchangeably the terms "subject," "substance," and "substantive" on the one hand, and "predicate," "attribute," and "quality" on the other hand. In the debate between Hobbes and Descartes, for example, presented in the *Third Set of Objections,* Hobbes

The Way We See the World

said that he agreed with Descartes and with "all philosophers" that we must distinguish "a subject . . . from its properties," but he disagreed that this subject was mental. Since "subjects . . . can be conceived only after a corporeal fashion," and since "we cannot separate thought from a matter that thinks, the proper inference seems to be that that which thinks is material rather than mental." To choose a more recent example, I notice that Strawson represents persons and their characteristics in the idioms appropriate to subjects and predicates. He rejects a "no-subject" doctrine like that of Hobbes, and he refers to persons as "subjects," to their material attributes as "material predicates," and to their mental states or experiences as "personal predicates."

HUME'S SKEPTICISM

The first step in questioning the traditional view is to point out that the commonsense division into substance and attribute is not as obvious as it appears. Every undergraduate student of philosophy is asked to try to become strange to the familiar and strip away in thought all the qualities from Berkeley's apple. Does he then believe that the substance of the apple remains? Certainly not. On the other hand, does he accept the next step? Does he believe with Berkeley that the apple is nothing but the combination of "its" qualities? Again, certainly not. Berkeley presented his argument in the clearest English, but the student immediately accepts the refutation presented in Dr. Johnson's far more powerful body-English of kicking the stone to refute Berkeley's doctrine, and he returns to the comfort of his earlier convictions.[5]

But the deepest skepticism of the first step is best seen in the case of Hume, the prominent skeptic of our era. Hume, in his *Treatise*, directs his attention to the substance-attribute conception itself.[6] We think of substance as "something which may exist by itself," and of attributes, properties, or qualities as entities "which cannot exist apart but require a subject of inhesion to sustain and support them." He applies this distinction to the customary examples of external substances (material bodies) and mental substances (minds or selves). Against our traditional conception, his main destructive argument is as follows: "When we talk of 'self' or 'substance' we must have an idea annexed to those terms, otherwise they are altogether unintelligible. Every idea is derived from preceding impressions; and we have no impression of self or substance as some thing simple and individual." In this fashion the complete triumph of skepticism, it might seem, was achieved by Hume. Unable to inspect material substance or to introspect mental substance ("we have no idea of substance of any kind"), he dropped substance as the defining feature of persons and things, as that feature that is customarily used to explain their numerical identity. His main constructive argument is as follows. Finding that he can never glimpse a physical object or catch himself "without some one or more perceptions," nor can he "perceive anything but the perceptions," he concludes: "It is the composition of these, therefore, which forms the self [or physical object]." His ulterior conclusion is that personal identity (as well as the identity of material objects) is an illusion to be explained in terms of the association of ideas. This skeptical ending of our traditional conception appears to give no way to distinguish one object from another or to distinguish myself from what is not myself. Hume's ultimate conclusion is a forlorn skepticism that he regards as a disease for which "carelessness and inattention alone can afford us any remedy." A total suspense of judgment is our only recourse.

The merit of this approach is that it exhibits an obvious way of destroying, to use Reid's words, "the reality of these distinctions" between substances and their attributes. It shows that substances are not observables or imaginables. Moreover, on its constructive side, it offers a suggestion for an alternative theory, namely, a "composition" theory of the self and of matter, which Hume, however, was reluctant to develop. The great weakness lies in Hume's literalism, manifested in his subscription to the *unum nomen unum nominatum* doctrine of meaning. The word "substance," he holds, is meaningless because it does not function as a proper name. This weakness parallels another. Hume holds that persons and things are nothing but bundles of perceptions, each perception being a discrete particular. A person, therefore, or a thing, is a bundle of particulars or substances, not a bundle of qualities or attributes. Presumably, any one of these particulars in the bundle is composed of other particulars or substances . . . and so on. Hume's maxim "Everything in nature is individual" has its counterpart in a naive theory of language that may be summarized, "Every term in language is a subject"; that is, Every term functions as a proper name. A final weakness appears when I elicit the hidden premise in Hume's argument. The latter, it will be agreed, is as follows: We have no idea of the subject or substance of the experiences, of that which has those experiences. We have, therefore, no idea of the self. Hence skepticism about the self is unavoidable. The missing first premise is: If we are to have the idea of the self, must we not have the idea of the subject or substance of experiences, of that which has the experiences? But, strangely enough, the first premise of

The Way We See the World

Hume's argument is basic to one who subscribes to our conceptual scheme. It is, in fact, accepted by Strawson, who expresses it as follows: "Yet to have the idea of himself, must he not have the idea of the subject of the experiences, of that which has them?"[7] Strawson, of course, unlike Hume, does not deny the consequent. Thus Hume, malgré lui, subscribes to the "reality" of the substance-attribute distinction. Here, then, is at least one example of Reid's contention that the skeptic eventually discloses his belief in the "reality" of this distinction.

RAMSEY'S SKEPTICISM

The second skeptical approach is more sophisticated. It consists in undermining the reality of the substance-attribute dichotomy by destroying its basis in the subject-predicate distinction. The best example of this approach and, indeed, almost the only one, is found in the work of F. P. Ramsey.[8] Ramsey discloses an "important assumption" made by previous theorists, one "which has not yet been thought of." "They assume," he claims, "a fundamental antithesis between subject and predicate." They assume that the subject and the predicate function in different ways. This, he argues, is a mistake. Taking the sentence "Socrates is wise" and turning it round to read "Wisdom is a characteristic of Socrates," Ramsey claims that both sentences "assert the same fact and express the same proposition." Which one we use is merely a matter of literary style or what happens to be our center of interest: Socrates or wisdom. Ramsey concludes that there is "no essential distinction" between subject and predicate and claims this "throws doubt upon the whole basis of the distinction between particular and universal as deduced from that between subject and predicate." He then makes the stronger claim that "the whole theory of particulars and universals is due to mistaking for a fundamental characteristic of reality what is merely a characteristic of language."

Ramsey's main argument against the claim that there is "a real difference" between subject and predicate is found, however, in his examination of *its* basis in the idea of "completeness" supposed to be present in subjects and absent in predicates. This idea had been developed by Russell in his *Philosophy of Logical Atomism* (1918) and was to be adopted later, as I have noted, by Strawson as "crucial." Russell had claimed that in order to understand a subject, that is, a name for a particular, such as "This" in "This is red," it is necessary only to "be acquainted with the particular"; whereas, in order to understand the predicate it is necessary to "know what is the meaning of saying that anything is red," that is, to "understand propositions of the form 'x is red'." Russell had claimed also that this distinction answers to the distinction between particulars, previously called "substances," and universals. "Each particular stands entirely alone and is completely self-subsistent," whereas universals are dependent entities.

Ramsey clarifies this idea of completeness. He points out that in the proposition "Socrates is wise," both the subject and predicate are incomplete since both involve the form of a proposition. Why, then, is "wise" more incomplete than "Socrates"? The explanation is that "Whereas with 'Socrates' we only have the idea of completing it in any manner into a proposition [any proposition in which 'Socrates' occurs], with 'wise' we have not only this but also an idea of completing it in a special way [a narrower collection of propositions of the form 'x is wise'], . . . which we may call its occurrence as predicate." But now Ramsey asks whether there is "a real difference." The answer he gives is that there is none. This is so because our decision to use substantives to define ranges of propositions in one way only is a matter of custom and of our common interests. We could use them as we now use adjectives. In which case the distinctions between "Socrates" and "wise," between subject and predicate, and accordingly, between substance and attribute or particular and universal, are "of a subjective character and depend on human interests and needs."

Ramsey's account has many merits. He shows that there is no "essential distinction," no "real difference," even in English, between subject and predicate. In this he corrects a traditional mistake. We saw that Reid, for example, accepted the "reality" of the distinction, and that Russell regarded predication as "ultimate." Ramsey shows that the distinction is of a "subjective" character depending upon human interests, for, of course, such distinctions are not found in the nature of things but are drawn by men in accordance with their interests, needs, or purposes. He shows that no fundamental division of objects into substances and attributes can be deduced from the distinction between subjects and predicates, for, of course, this would indeed be an extreme case of worshipping Bacon's Idol of the Market Place. It would be mistaking what is merely a feature of language for a fundamental feature of the world. Finally, following Whitehead, Ramsey offers a suggestion for an alternative theory of the nature of material objects, according to which they are construed neither as subjects owning predicates, as in the traditional doctrine, nor as discrete subjects without any predicates, as in Hume's theory, but as "adjectives of events."

The Way We See the World

The grave weakness in Ramsey's account echoes the equally grave weakness in Hume's which I called his "literalism." This weakness is of the same order as "fundamentalism" in the philosophy of religion and "essentialism" in the philosophy of science. Both Hume and Ramsey reject the substance-attribute dichotomy but for different reasons. Hume looks for the direct evidence. He rejects the dichotomy because he cannot find that elusive substance. He might just as well reject the idea of Santa Claus because, after waiting up all night, he cannot find that elusive bringer of gifts. Hume thus represents the first skeptic in my account of the rejection of Plato's myth. Finding no direct evidence for the belief in the class structure, he rejects the belief as false and the structure itself as unreal. Ramsey's reason is the more interesting. He examines the indirect evidence. Assuming that the substance-attribute distinction is deduced from the subject-predicate distinction, he argues that since there is no essential distinction between the subject and the predicate, we must give up the substance-attribute distinction and, with it, what he refers to as "that great muddle, the theory of universals." Ramsey thus represents the approach of the second skeptic. He assumes that the distinction between classes is based upon the distinction between metals in the makeup of the members of the community. Then, having performed several autopsies upon members all scrupulously conducted, and having found no real difference between them, Ramsey concludes that all class distinctions must be abolished.

THE TWO MODELS

Standing on the shoulders of these two remarkable men, I hope to profit from their great insights as well as from their mistakes. The obvious features of my hypothesis are clearly seen when it is set up as a rival to the traditional conception represented in its extreme form by the statement of Thomas Reid, the philosopher of common sense. This uncritical acceptance of the "reality" of the doctrine resembles the subscription to the now discarded doctrines of innate ideas, of nativism in optics, and, more recently, of the steady state doctrine of the universe. It is taken for granted that the doctrine, far from being the invention of philosophers, is common to all men and found in the structure of all languages. Anybody who questions it is labeled "skeptic" by members within the establishment. According to my rival hypothesis, on the other hand, the reality of the distinctions in question is replaced by their subjectivity and relativity; they are seen as the brilliant speculations or inventions of men of genius. These inventions were applied to the allocation of the objects of the world of our experience, to the classification of material objects and of persons, and, of course, to the structuring of the way we talk about these things.

Some of the not-so-obvious features of my hypothesis emerge when I elicit the not-so-obvious rivalry between my view and that of Ramsey. The latter argues that we must relinquish the distinction between substance and attribute because there is no real difference between subject and predicate on which it is based; and this in turn is true because subjects are just as incomplete as predicates. But we might just as well or just as badly argue that we must relinquish the conclusion of an argument because its premise is false. It might be the case that there is a real difference between substance and attribute although there is none between subject and predicate. According to my hypothesis, on the other hand, the vocabulary of "real" and "essential," used to qualify the two distinctions, is dropped. Both distinctions, when their features are expressed, are treated as different theories, one about the world, the other about language; in which case they are tested by those canons customarily used to test any scientific theory, not by their premises (as Ramsey tests the traditional doctrine), although these may be clarified, but by their consequences. In the present case, however, two theories are obviously very closely related: they are not competing or rival theories, but one is an auxiliary of the other with an overlapping or common structure. Accordingly, one of them, the subject-predicate distinction, is appropriately treated as a model for the other.

Here I use two definitions of "model," apparently conflicting. In the first, a model is an extended and sustained metaphor, one in which the features of the metaphor are specified; a metaphor is a representation of the facts of one sort in the idioms appropriate to another. These ideas I developed some time ago.[9] In the second, a model is just another theory, an alternative interpretation of the one skeleton or calculus. These two definitions represent merely two points of view corresponding to two time-honored ways of teaching or of persuading an audience. Invented by the Greeks as the best ways of delivering science, they are the analytical and the synthetical procedures. They mark "the difference," in Aristotle's words, "between arguments to and from the first principles," respectively. In the first, we commonly make use of models. Models help us make discoveries by suggesting ways to extend what will be our theory. Thus Plato in his *Republic*, that paradigm of the use of paradigms, uses the model of the state to help him make discoveries about the nature of man. All of this is based upon the original metaphor present in "Man is a state." Plato uses several features of the vehicle of the metaphor to illustrate corresponding features in the freight. In the second, the model, like any scaffolding after it has done its job, is dispensed with. The scientist merely presents his theory. Had Plato presented his account as a system, all the politics, being redundant, would have been omitted. Probably, however, as in other cases, some of the vocabulary of politics would have rubbed off onto his psychology in some such form as "Reason rules," "Spirit guards," and so on. In accordance with the second definition of model, Plato's students at the Academy might have tried to reconstruct the two theories, interpreting the symbols of the calculus to produce a theory of man and a theory of states.

Since the *Republic* is a work in analysis—that is, an essay *toward* a new theory of man, not the presentation of one—it exhibits the apparatus that Plato used and thus the features of his model or paradigm alongside the corresponding features of the thing modeled. The student finds no difficulty in seeing the parallels. But there was no corresponding book for the student of our present subject. If one had been available in the West shortly after the invention of the notions of subject-predicate and substance-attribute, posterity might not have accepted without question that there is only one way to see the world. The parallels might always have been obvious, and Ramsey might not have written in 1925 of the assumption of the subject-predicate antithesis as something "which has not yet been thought of." Instead, philosophers have applied the substance-attribute conception to the solution of concrete problems. Only recently have they tried to reconstruct the two domains and to exhibit the model alongside the theory. This is not easy, because the vocabularies of the two domains have been mixed. We encounter statements comparable to "Reason rules" and "Spirit guards." Fortunately, we do have a substitute for the book corresponding to the *Republic*. This substitute is found in the various writings of Aristotle, who may have been the first to draw the two distinctions and to make use of the main parallels between them. In his writings, however, the vocabularies of the two domains are already mixed. Two characteristic passages are these: "A subject [*to hypokeimenon*, thing underlying] is that about which anything is predicated but which is not itself predicated of anything else. . . . To be a subject seems really to be the first meaning of substance [ousia]" (*Metaphysics* 1028b); and "Some things are universal, others particular. By the term 'universal' [to katholon] I mean that which is of such a nature as to be predicated of many subjects; by 'particular' that which is not thus predicated. Thus 'man' is a universal, 'Callias' a particular" (*De Interpretatione* 7). To summarize from these and other passages, we can elicit the main parallels between language and ontology that entered our conceptual scheme. The paradigm of a subject-predicate statement is one in which a proper noun is joined to an adjective by the copula or the "is" of predication, as in "Socrates is wise." The subject or substantive, rendered in Greek or Latin, carries the suggestion of lying under as a support, while the predicate, represented by the adjective (etymologically "adjunct," and elliptical for *adjectivum verbum* or "added word") carries the suggestion of incompleteness and dependence. Thus we have the unkind reference to the Scots as "those Northern adjectives not able to exist without [the substantive] England." We notice that the same predicate can be ascribed to many subjects and that many predicates can be ascribed to the same subject. It is easy to see how well these features can be used to model the basic features of our world. There are substances or particulars that are the primary existents represented by persons and material objects. They are supposed to be self-subsistent, independent entities. Their attributes or universals, the secondary existents, have only an "adjectival" existence. They require a substance to support them. We notice that the same universal has many instances, that is, is present in many substances, and that many universals can be present in one substance. We notice also that Aristotle spoiled the symmetry between the two distinctions. Although he said that a subject can never be a predicate, he indicated that a predicate can be a subject; for example, " 'Animal' is predicated of the species 'man' " (*Categories* 5). Certainly this is what we do. We make nouns out of adjectives and treat them as subjects. Nevertheless, it produces a feature we do not want in the model, for when we draw the parallel we find that universals, along with concrete individuals like Socrates, are substances. Accordingly, Aristotle treated them as secondary substances.

The history of science records many instances in which the model is modified to fit the theory. Aristotle himself modified Eudoxus' model of the spheres to fit his own theory. The present case is yet another instance. Here the model has since been repaired but at the expense of some damage done to ordinary language. Russell showed how to repair the model. He argued that a predicate can never stand alone. "When it *seems* to occur as a subject, the phrase needs amplifying and explaining." Thus Artistotle's "Man is an animal" is analyzed into two sentential functions "(x) (if x is a man, then x is an animal)," in which each function keeps the subject-predicate form and the trespassing "man" is restored to its proper place, namely, to the predicate.[10] In this way, adopted generally by logicians, the symmetry between model and theory was preserved.

By thus eliciting the main parallels between the two conceptions, I am able, to some extent, to become strange to the familiar, to take off, as it were, and examine the spectacles I have worn for so long without knowing I had them on. Like the third skeptic, I am able to return to a point of view similar to that of Plato with respect to his invention of the Myth of the Earth-Born and to refer to the Subject-Predicate Myth.

We notice at once, however, that although Plato invented the Myth of the Earth-Born as a device to explain and reinforce belief in the class structure, he regarded the class structure of his republic as a device calculated to illustrate and help him work out his theory of man. Plato might have said that he had invented two myths, the Myth of the Earth-Born and the Myth of the Republic, or, more appropriately, two models or paradigms, one of which functioned as an auxiliary of the other. We notice a similar structure in our present subject matter. While working toward a theory of universals we distinguish between the statements of what will be our theory and the statements of our subject-predicate model. We do this just as we distinguish between the literal and the metaphorical relative to or within the context of our purposes and interests, or in relation to ordinary language. But there is surely nothing fixed or absolute about it. Within another context the theory may be used as a model. We may use the subject-predicate distinction as an auxiliary for the substance-attribute model to illustrate the nature of man just as Plato used the state model and its auxiliary. Within this context we notice that to speak of persons as *substances* or *subjects* owning *attributes,* or possessing *characteristics,* or as subjects to which we *ascribe* certain *predicates,* is to speak in metaphor. By taking this position I adopt most of the features that I ascribed to the third skeptic, and I return to a point of view no more revolutionary than Plato's.

In the position of the third skeptic I drop the notion that the substance-attribute distinction is fundamental to the world. I drop also the parallel notion that the subject-predicate distinction is a fundamental feature of language. In this I am in agreement first with Hume and Ramsey and then with Ramsey. Countering them, I hold that the distinction, if useful, may be restored; also that it is to be tested not directly or by examining its basis but by its consequences in application to concrete problems of mind and matter. Thus I reveal a fundamental difference between my approach and Strawson's in his *Individuals*. The problem in the philosophy of mind that Strawson tries to solve he presents in a Kantian style: Given that we can and do identify persons—that is, we distinguish one person, including ourselves, from others—what is the nature of persons presupposed by this fact? Or what conception of a person *must* we hold?[11] His solution is an extended application of the subject-predicate model. In one passage, already quoted, he summarizes his solution: [In order for any person] "to have the idea of himself must he not have the idea of the subject of the experiences, of that which has them?" Although Strawson uses the same subject-predicate model as did Descartes and his followers, his interpretation of it is different. Descartes conceived a person as a composition of two substances, mental and material, each owning its own mental and material attributes. Because he sees Descartes as forced into solipsism, Strawson conceives a person as one subject owning both mental and material predicates. In this fashion, Strawson gives his solution to the problem of personal identification: A person must own observable material predicates; otherwise we could not distinguish him from others.

Although I have said that the theories of Descartes and Strawson represent two of the many different applications of the same model or paradigm, it should be noted that such idioms as "model," "paradigm," "analogy," and the like are foreign to these philosophers' accounts. Descartes, although he used such terms as "subject" and "substance," may have been unaware even of the existence of the parallel between grammar and ontology. Strawson, on the other hand, although he uses interchangeably such terms as the grammatical "subject" and the ontological "particular," is fully aware of the parallel. His exhibition of the two sides of the parallel constitutes a main merit of his account, enabling us to perceive the presence of either a weak or a strong analogy or to tell whether the vehicle can carry its freight. But for Strawson the parallel between the subject-predicate distinction and the substance-attribute or particular-universal dichotomy is more than an analogy or model. The presence of a model suggests and allows for the possibility of an alternative model, but Strawson's argument—according to which, if we have the idea of a person, then we must have the idea of a subject of experience—manifests the same a priori character as does that of Descartes. Perhaps, then, while we should adopt Strawson's starting point (the facts as they are commonly agreed to be) we should ask not "What theory must we hold?" but rather "What theory provides the best explanation?"

CONCLUSION: A WEAKNESS IN SUBJECT-PREDICATE THEORIES OF MIND

The subject-predicate dichotomy and the parallel substance-attribute distinction have been of enormous utility; otherwise they would not have endured. Perhaps, however, there is no need to adopt the subject-predicate model. Maybe in this time of change we should look afresh at these fundamental conceptions. There are other ways of seeing the world, other ways of "allocating the facts."

Let me for the time being consider one feature of the theories of mind based upon these two models. I note especially an imbalance with regard to activity and passivity. If a mind is a subject or substance, then it is a complete, independent being, a substratum that stands under as a support for other entities. If subject or substance lies under, or stands under, as the etyma indicate, thus leading to the concept of the *Understanding*, it carries no suggestion of power or agency, only of passivity. It does suggest giving support as pillars do to a building, but there is no activity or agency in a pillar. Anything active or possessing power or agency does not, therefore, fit well as a subject according to the model. Accordingly, any power or agency is relegated to the predicates or attributes owned by the subject or substance.

What, then, of these predicates or attributes? We have noted that these are incomplete entities dependent for their existence on the substantial subject that supports them. Yet, among these unsubstantial attributes, we find all the active features that we usually regard as integral to minds or persons: willing, causing, and creating. It is no wonder that within our Cartesian-Newtonian tradition, the dominant picture of the human mind offered by the philosophers is that of a passive observer receiving impressions from the outside world. This is seen, for example in the solutions of the great philosophers to the problems of vision and perception they were so fond of addressing. Whereas in truth our era has been one of the most creative, productive, and destructive periods in history. The correspondingly creative aspect of our minds has not been well served by this model.

In case we have gone off the track, let us return to the remote past, to an era preceding that of the invention of the subject-predicate, substance-attribute models. Let us return to the contributions of Plato and Aristotle to find, if possible, the origins of our traditional doctrine.

CHAPTER 2

Exposing the Root Metaphor:
Plato's Androgynous Cosmos

The greatest thing by far is to be a master of metaphor.

Aristotle

In this chapter I use my interpretation of Plato's *Timaeus* to elicit the bases of our traditional views about the mind, found in two root metaphors of Western thought: the Procreation Model and the Craftsman Model. The former furnishes us with such conceptions as passive and active, a receptacle, stuff or "matter" (from the Greek *meter*, mother), creator, and child resulting from the intercourse of father and mother. The Craftsman Model provides us with conceptions of constructor, of material (Aristotle's word for matter is *hyle*, the wood of the craftsman), and of product. Although these metaphors subsequently are used to illustrate the structure and operations of the mind, Plato also uses them in his *Timaeus* to set up theories of the creation and structure of the cosmos.

I offer a new perspective on the *Timaeus*, a strange and fascinating work, so enigmatic that it challenges the student to identify its nature and purpose. Is it intended as a work on cosmology or on physiology?

The reader may puzzle over why I go into such detail to solve the riddle of the *Timaeus* when all I seek is the origin of the substance-attribute model of the mind. The answer lies in my introductory comments on the metaphorical way. Exposing the nature of a more than half-hidden metaphor is a problem of peculiar interest and difficulty. Searching for the beginnings of the substance-attribute theory, I began picking up tantalizing clues toward a solution to the riddle of the *Timaeus*, the big clue being hidden in Plato's fantastic appendix. Once I possessed this clue, much of the *Timaeus* became clear to me. I suggest that you read or reread Plato's *Timaeus*, together with this chapter, to see it from this point of view. It is a very small book, easy to read, and one that has had enormous influence on Western civilization.

PLATO'S FANTASTIC APPENDIX

In the last two pages of the *Timaeus*, Plato, having completed the task laid down at the outset, "to tell the story of the universe down to the generation of man," adds an account of the manner in which other animals have come into being. He first explains the origin of the difference between the sexes, following with a physiological and psychological account of human procreation, beginning with "the love of sexual intercourse" and ending with the birth of the child. Recent commentators either ignore this passage or treat it lightly. A. E. Taylor, for example, says that Plato presents it in an "unmistakably playful" fashion and that "we must not take what Timaeus says about these matters too seriously,"[1] while F. M. Cornford notes that the whole passage is "fantastic," and this because the sexual organs are described as living creatures.[2] These commentators, of course, are correct in what they notice: the passage is playful and fantastic. But then, so is the whole *Timaeus*. They fail to notice that this is serious play, the significance of which is fantastic. They miss, it seems to me, its astonishing parallels with the body of the work. Accordingly, the hypothesis I propose to develop is that in this appendix Plato discloses a guiding idea or root metaphor of the *Timaeus*.

THE NATURE OF THE TIMAEUS

In order to do this, we must be clear on what the *Timaeus* is primarily about. This is difficult, for although the *Timaeus* may have been Plato's most influential book, it is also one of the most obscure, probably intentionally so.[3] Unlike much of Plato's work, it is riddled with oracular utterances rather than reasoned arguments and presented as science fiction or "likely myth" rather than scientific truth. It is as if Plato seeks to hide his message from the uninitiated by presenting it in code. Unlike much of Plato's work, it was not for popular presentation but for the instruction of the few, a work of seventy-five pages in which, after an apparently irrelevant summary account of the Ideal State, actualized as ancient Athens and the defeat of Atlantis, Plato tries to coordinate the findings of several sciences ranging from geometry, physics, astronomy, and optics in Parts I and II to anatomy, physiology, and pathology in Part III.

Ostensibly, the *Timaeus* is a work in cosmogony and cosmology using the model of geometry. These subjects not only occupy the bulk of the book but dominate the first two parts, which deal with the geometrical construction of the world. They have been called by Karl Popper "Plato's greatest achievement," and have had enormous influence on the development of modern science.[4] They provided, as Popper points out, an "intellectual tool-box" for a long line of physicists from Aristarchus through Galileo and Kepler to Newton and Einstein. Part III, with its crude anatomy, physiology, and pathology, if noticed at all, is regarded as of secondary importance.

This traditional view becomes suspect, however, once one grasps the nature of Plato's teaching methods and the devices he uses. Subscribers to this view of the *Timaeus* have fallen into the trap of concluding that because a subject is primary in Plato's pedagogical sequence and occupies the bulk of his work, it must be the primary subject. One of Plato's favorite teaching devices is the extended metaphor or model. The words he uses to refer to this device are *eikon* and *paradeigma*. In the *Politicus* he stresses this point: "It is difficult," he says, "to set forth anything of real importance except through the medium of the metaphor or model [*paradeigma*]" (277D). Later in the same work he offers a definition: "We take something that is less well known and compare it with something else that is better known, so that out of the comparison there arises one true notion which includes both of them" (278C).[5] On many occasions Plato shows by example how the metaphorical method works. Some of the best examples are in the *Republic* and the *Timaeus*, two works not usually considered together.[6] Nevertheless, Plato himself considers them together in the opening of the *Timaeus:* "Yesterday" Socrates discussed the Ideal State, and "today" Timaeus discusses the cosmos. Moreover, these works have roughly the same structure, and their contents are complementary. We can use the *Republic* as a paradigm for the *Timaeus*.

Although an author proposes, posterity disposes. On the face of it, the *Republic* is primarily about politics, just as the *Timaeus* is primarily about cosmology. It seems to me, however, that posterity has misread both works in much the same manner, just as Julian Marias describes in his account of how we are prone to misread metaphor: "The role of metaphor is like my finger when I point to something. When I point to something, I am suggesting that you look in this direction in order to discover what I am seeing. I am not suggesting you look at my finger. Some people do. And this is very surprising. Unfortunately this also happens in philosophy!"[7] When we consider the deeper structure of the *Republic* and the *Timaeus*, we find that posterity has been looking at Plato's finger, in one case at the politics, in the other at the cosmology.

Plato's Androgynous Cosmos

But Plato is pointing to something else. These two works are pristine treatises in the science of man, the one in psychology and ethics (the diseases and health of the psyche), the other in physiology and medicine (the diseases and health of the body). Accordingly, the long opening accounts of the ideal polis and the "real" cosmos are merely secondary subjects, that is, Plato's teaching devices. They are the vehicles of extended metaphors or models: "likely myths," invented by Plato to elucidate the features of his primary subjects that complement one another. In the *Republic*, Plato introduces the "large letters" of the polis in order to teach his audience how to read the smaller letters of man. In the *Timaeus*, without disclosing that he does so, Plato uses once more the device of the "large letters," this time of the cosmos, to teach his students something different about man as the primary subject. The sequence of the two works is roughly the same: In the *Republic*, Socrates begins with the origin of the state and ends with the nature of man. In the other, "Timaeus will begin with the origin of the cosmos and end with the nature of man" (27A). The two different metaphors, "Man is a micropolis" and "Man is a microcosm," illuminate different aspects of the same subject. In the *Republic*, Plato, like any scientist using a model, specifies without argument three parts in the model polis: the ruling, the executive, and the artisan classes, and names their corresponding virtues. Then he deduces parallel parts in the thing modeled, the human soul: reason, spirit, and appetite, and confirms their presence by independent testing. Finally, he elicits their corresponding virtues: wisdom, courage, and self-restraint, with justice as a harmonious relationship of the three parts of the soul. In the *Timaeus*, although the "real" cosmos replaces the "ideal" polis, Plato uses essentially the same method.

	The Model Macropolis			The Theory Micropolis	
Parts	Virtues		Parts	Virtues	
Ruling	Wisdom	⎫	Reason	Wisdom	⎫
Executive	Courage	⎬ JUSTICE	Spirit	Courage	⎬ JUSTICE
	Self-	⎭		Self-	⎭
Artisan	Restraint		Appetite	Restraint	

Fig. 2.1 Man as a micropolis: *Republic* II–V

In Part I, he exhibits the "surface" structure of the model cosmos and sketches its parallels in the human soul and body. In Part II he reveals the "deep" structure of the cosmos, showing how to construct, from two elementary triangles, four of the five regular solids, leaving the fifth, the dodecahedron, unconstructed. Next, he elicits the four corresponding "elements" of fire, air, water, and earth, with the fifth, aether, that is implicitly present and explains particular phenomena as combinations of these. In Part III, Plato uses his model to exhibit the structure of the human body, to describe the functions of its parts, and to correlate these parts with the parts of the soul and their virtues previously isolated in the *Republic*. This enables him to conclude with accounts in pathology and therapeutics, which concern not only the body but also the soul.

This summary of Plato's teaching sequence and method suggests the *Timaeus* is what amounts to an interdisciplinary study. It suggests also that the last part of the "course" is of first importance to Plato, for it contains his primary subject. If this is so, Plato today might be accused of meddling outside his profession. The particular subjects covered in Part III—anatomy, physiology, pathology, and therapeutics, with an appendix on genetics—are the central topics for a course in medicine and suggest that the *Timaeus* is primarily a manual for medical students.[8] Further explanation of why, in the West, at least until the late middle ages, posterity fixed its gaze upon Plato's "finger" is that schol-

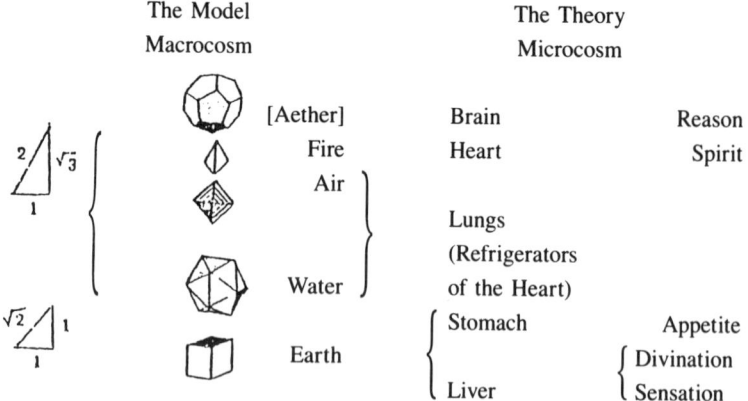

Fig. 2.2. Man as a microcosm: *Timaeus* 53C–61C, 69C–72D, 73CD. The lungs, "receiving breath and drink, serve to cool the heart, and give rest and relief from the burning heat" (70C). They thus serve to temper the spirited element.

Plato's Androgynous Cosmos

ars lacked an account of what Plato was pointing at. The only version of the *Timaeus* readily available was the fourth-century Latin translation of *Chalcidius*.[9] This contains only pages 17–53c, that is, only the first half of the book, and thus omits all the medical subjects. Accordingly, Plato's image then as now was that of Raphael's fresco in the Vatican depicting the venerable philosopher holding a copy of the *Timaeus* in one hand while pointing to the heavens with the other. The "other Plato" is perhaps better known in the Byzantine tradition as represented in the eleventh-century painting of "Plato receiving medical lore from Aesculapius and Chiron."[10]

We can now glimpse part of the machinery that Plato uses to coordinate diverse disciplines. There are two connecting links. The first is Plato's ulterior purpose, which all the disciplines covered are made to serve, as they do in the case of the medical subjects in Part III. Plato's guiding of his students through the latest findings in medical science culminates in an account of the best therapy for the body and mind. It is not so easily seen that the same is true of the nonmedical subjects covered in Parts I and II. Thus the second coordinating device is the model or extended metaphor that, by definition, is a sort-crossing instrument. The medical students are taught to view the soul and body through the spectacles of the cosmos. They learn, for example, that some diseases of the body have their counterparts in the "diseases" of the model, the wandering motions of parts of the cosmos, and that the best medicine for the diseases of the mind and body is to imitate the motions of different parts of the universe (88E). But the cosmology and cosmogony themselves require another metaphor. The students are taught to view their physics and astronomy through the spectacles of geometry. They learn, to choose just one example, that the key to the physics of the cosmos is the simple, continuous, geometrical proportion: $A:B = B:C = C:D$ (for example, fire:air = air:water = water:earth).

THE CRAFTSMAN MODEL

There is yet a deeper structure to the *Timaeus*. The preceding account was concerned with Plato's pedagogical devices. What were his aids to discovery? If Plato was using the geometrical model of the cosmos as a device for teaching others, was there a model that he used to teach himself? The question can be asked in the terms of the opening section of Part I of the *Timaeus:* In order to construct this cosmos, the Demiurge first fixed his gaze upon an eternal model (*paradeigma*), a composite Form, and then proceeded to make a copy of it (28A). But on

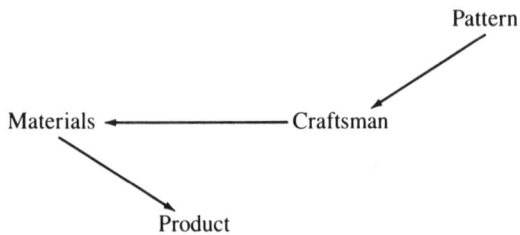

Fig. 2.3. The Craftsman Model: *Timaeus* 28A, 60

what model or models did Plato fix *his* gaze in order to develop his account of this construction?

The first answer, I suppose, is that Plato fixed his gaze upon the same eternal Form as did the Demiurge. But this is unlikely, since Plato, like us, was probably more familiar with concrete things in time than with abstract ideas outside it. More likely Plato had before his mind's eye the concrete model of ordinary craftsmanship, in which a craftsman, equipped with a set-square and expert knowledge of applied geometry, constructs an intricate artificial object out of materials from a pattern or plan. Such an answer would be generally accepted, for commentators talk almost exclusively of the Demiurge and his geometrical constructions. It accords also with the traditional view of the nature of the *Timaeus* and with the account just given of Plato's teaching devices and sequence; moreover it is so obvious. On the surface, Part I of the *Timaeus* shows that the Craftsman Model dominates Plato's thought and certainly is his main teaching device. Plato actually says that he has described "the works wrought by the craftsmanship of intelligence" (47E).

THE PROCREATION MODEL

Nevertheless, every teacher or scientist knows that the models or examples used to illustrate points or theories are often different from the models used to work them out and that the teaching sequence rarely follows the sequence of discoveries. Even in Part I, the citadel of the Craftsman Model, we detect, only partially submerged, the presence of another model, that of Procreation. We learn that: the Maker or Cause of the cosmos is not only a craftsman but also a father (28C, 37C, 41A); the cosmos was "generated" as an "animal" endowed with "soul and reason," containing "all other animals"; the Model Form, also, is an "animal," albeit a "perfect" one; this cosmos "closely resembles" not

Plato's Androgynous Cosmos

only the Model Form but also the Cause; and the Model Form "cannot have a double" (29E–31A). These disclosures in Part I reveal some defects in the Craftsman Model in relation to Plato's finished theory. Even in Plato's day it was difficult for a craftsman to construct a living animal in his workshop. The disclosures reveal that Plato envisages between the Maker of the cosmos and the Model Form a relation far more intimate than that between a craftsman and his pattern. They reveal, moreover, a grave omission in Plato's overt references to the Procreation Model: The father needs a mother in order to produce an animal. Finally, these disclosures suggest that since the cosmos is an animal that is generated, and since its parts are animals, the *Timaeus* might have been called *Generation of Animals*.[11]

In Part II Plato repairs these defects and corrects the omission. He begins by introducing a new entity, Necessity, with the suggestion of a new relationship between the maker and the cosmos: "The generation of this cosmos came about through a combination of Necessity and Intelligence: the two commingled" (48A). He then introduces the Wandering

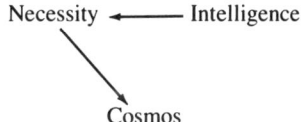

Fig. 2.4. The combination of Necessity and Intelligence: *Timaeus* 48A

Cause, the Receptacle, and the Nurse of the cosmos, and he discovers primitive entities more basic than earth, air, fire, and water. These are the two elementary triangles *out of which* the body of the world is made. What are the natures and the roles of these new entities, and how are they related? For the first time Plato discloses what appear to be the main features of his second model: the mother, the father, and the child.

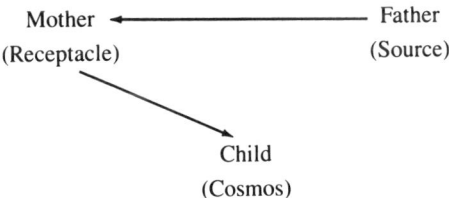

Fig. 2.5. The Procreation Model: *Timaeus* 50CD

The mother is the Receptacle *in which* the child is born, the father is the source *from which* the child "is copied and begotten," and their child is the cosmos (50DC). But just as the so-called elements (earth, air, fire, and water) are not the primitives or letters of Plato's system (48C), so the mother, father, and child are not the primitives or letters of his second model. Plato does not reveal those primitives here.

It seems to me that Plato spells out the letters of his model not in the body of the *Timaeus* but, almost as if it were an afterthought, in the appendix:

> The gods created in us the desire for sexual intercourse, fashioning one kind of animate nature in men, and another in women. The two were made by them in this way. What we drink makes its way through the lungs into the kidneys and thence the bladder from which it is expelled by air pressure. From this channel they bored a hole into the column of marrow which runs from the head down the neck and along the spine and has, indeed, in our earlier discourse been called 'semen.' This, being quick with soul and finding an outlet, gave to the part where it found the outlet a lively appetite for emission and produced a love of procreating. Hence it is that in men the genital organ becoming rebellious and self-willed, like an animal that will not listen to reason, and maddened with the sting of lust, seeks to gain absolute sway. In women also, what is called the matrix and womb, a living nature within them desirous of child-bearing, if it is left unfruitful long beyond the proper time, is vexed and aggrieved, and wandering throughout the body and blocking the channels of the breath by preventing respiration brings the sufferer to extreme distress and causes all manner of disorders; until at last the eros of one and the desire of the other bring the pair together, pluck as it were the fruit from the living tree and sow in the womb, as in a field, living things as yet unformed and too small to be seen, which take shape and are nourished until they grow large within; after which they are born into the light of day and thus the generation of animals is completed (91A–D).

Let me extract the main features of Plato's model with the help of Aristotle's *Generation of Animals,* written about thirty years later and itself an expansion of this appendix. I assume that much of the material in Aristotle's work was available and would have been familiar to Plato.

The womb is the embodiment of female desire (*epithumia*), "the desire of child-bearing." Plato uses two names for it (*meta* and *hystera*), perhaps in order to elicit its two roles, like our two meanings for "nurse": the wet = to suckle or nourish, and the dry = to cradle, as in Lady Macbeth's "I have given suck and know how sweet it is to tend the babe that milks me. . . . " These two roles of cradling and nourishing

Plato's Androgynous Cosmos   31

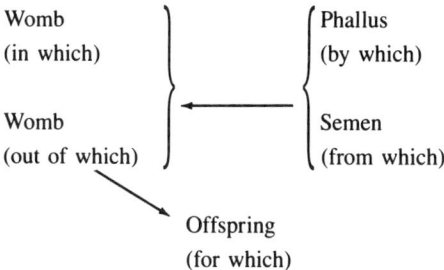

Fig. 2.6. The Procreation Model: *Timaeus* 91A–D

are exhibited in Plato's use of the preposition "in," the adverb "within," and the prefix "out of." He says that living things are sown "in the womb" (*eis metram*) and that, while there, they are "*nourished out of* [some nutriment] within [*entos ekthrepsontai*]." We learn from elsewhere that the nutriment (*trophos*) is blood (*haima*), "streams of which course through the whole body" (80D, 81A). If unfulfilled, the womb goes wandering (*planomenon*) throughout the body. Plato's account follows that of Hippocrates, who in his *Sicknesses of Women* coined the word *hysteria* and ascribed it to the wandering womb: When women are deprived of sexual relations, the uterus dries up and wanders throughout the body in search of moisture.[12] According to Aristotle, "Essentially the female is that which can generate in itself [*eis auto*] and out of which [*ex hou*] comes the offspring . . . " (16A); and "The female provides the material [*hyle*] for generation, and this is in the substance of the menstrual fluid [*katamenia*]" (27B).

The phallus is the embodiment and symbol of the male eros, "an eros of begetting." Plato uses the word *aidoia,* derived from the adjective *aidoios:* "regarded with awe or reverence."

The semen (*sperma*) is referred to earlier as "the divine seed" (*theion sperma*) implanted in that portion of the marrow called "brain," the seat also of the immortal soul and man's special daemon (*daimona*), or genius or anima, man being an inverted tree with the spinal column as the trunk and the brain as its roots in the sky (69C, 73C, 90A,C). The spherical head housing these divine entities is the microcosmic counterpart of the ring of stars "cosmetically arranged round the circle of heaven" (40A, 44D). In the *Phaedo* (109B) the heaven is called "aether," and in the *Epinomis* (981f) Plato, or a disciple, makes explicit that the fifth substance, corresponding to the dodecahedron, is aether. Aristotle develops some of these points. He says that "what the male contributes to generation is the form and efficient cause'' (29A); and that "the semen contains within itself that which causes it to be fertile—what is known as 'hot' substance, which is not fire or any similar force, but the *pneuma* which is enclosed within the semen or foam-like stuff (*aphrodes*) . . . after which the goddess who is supreme in matters of sexual intercourse was called'' (36AB). Then he says that "this *pneuma* (or spirit) is analogous to the element that belongs to the stars'' (36B). From his *De Caelo* we learn that this element is aether, the so-called quintessence, that its motion is circular, and that it is ungenerated, indestructible, and divine (269A–269B).

The offspring at conception in the womb are unformed (*adiaplasta*), too small to be seen, awaiting formation and nourishment.

PROCREATION AS A MODEL FOR THE COSMOS

Let me try to project the root ideas from Plato's short account of human procreation on to his cosmogony and, in part, on to his cosmology. The second sentence of Part II of the *Timaeus*, already quoted, continues with the personification of Intelligence and Necessity: "Intelligence, controlling Necessity, persuaded her to lead to the best end the most part of the things coming into existence, and thereby it came about through Necessity surrendering to intelligent persuasion . . . '' (48A). Considerable obscurity surrounds this and subsequent statements that seem to be somewhere between metaphorical and theoretical. The vocabulary is mixed, accounting in part for the difficulties in understanding the nature of the main items in Plato's system. How, for example, is space related to matter? Is matter present at all? Aristotle says that "Plato, in the *Timaeus*, identifies matter and space'' (*Physics*, 209B). But is not matter absent from Plato's system, just as his account lacks the technical word *hyle* coined for it by Aristotle? According to Cornford, "we are to get rid of the notion of material substance.''[13] How are the basic triangles related to matter and the Forms and these, in turn, to the Maker or Demiurge?

There are five main items in Plato's system modeled upon the essential features of the intercourse between female and male and its product. The question How is space related to matter? reduces first to the question How is the Receptacle related to the Nurse (in one sense of the word)? and this, in turn, to the question, How is the womb related to the materials in it?

In introducing his account of the Receptacle, Plato uses two different names, "the Receptacle, and, as it were, the Nurse of all becoming''

Plato's Androgynous Cosmos 33

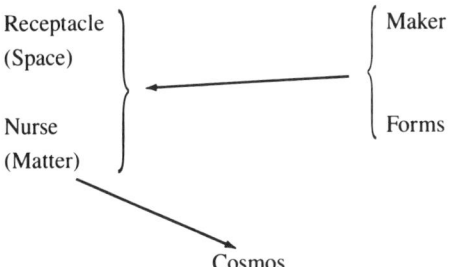

Fig. 2.7. The birth of the cosmos: *Timaeus* 27A, 48A–53B

(49A), corresponding to his two words for the womb, the *metra* and the *hystera*. Also he assigns it two different properties defined by his use of the two key prepositions "in which" and "out of which." The first is that of being a cradle or container, later called "space" (*chora*) in which (*en ho*) the cosmos comes to be, while the second is that of giving nourishment, subsequently called "matter" (from *mater*, mother, or *metra*, womb) out of which (*ex ho*) the cosmos is formed. These properties correspond to Plato's distinction between a dry nurse and wet nurse (88D; cf. *Republic* 373C, 460D). Accordingly, Aristotle's remark that Plato identifies matter and space is true only if Plato failed to distinguish the Receptacle from the Nurse, that is, the role of cradling from that of nourishing. However, Aristotle continues by stating that Plato corrected himself in his *Unwritten Teachings* by identifying place (*topos*) and space, and then proceeds to present a view much the same as Plato's: "Place seems to be like a receptacle . . . which is no part of that which is in it . . . and as the body's container, place differs from the body's material" (*Physics* 209B).

The material out of which the cosmos is fashioned is indeterminate substance in a state of "discordant and disorderly motion." It is referred to as "the Wandering Cause" and as "Necessity," indicating a hypothetical pre-existent chaos, modeled on the wandering womb. As in the *Republic*, Plato presents his account as if it were historical, in terms of origins. This partially hides his logical or physiological account in terms of primitives or stuff out of which the present world is constantly created. What are these primitives? He rejects the view of the early physicists that the elements or "letters" of physics are earth, air, fire, and water. These, he claims, are not even "syllables" (48B). His own hypothesis is that the letters or primitives of physics, the ultimate stuff out of which the things of this world are made are the two sorts of elementary triangles (53D). On the face of it, these triangles are unlikely candidates for the role of primitive matter. Matter is indeterminate, formless substance, while triangles are paragons of form and order and should be instruments of the Demiurge for imposing form on matter. This difficulty in interpreting the *Timaeus* admits of solution when we look at it through the Procreation Model. There are, as it were, material triangles as well as formal and actual ones. The material provided by the female is formless until impregnated by the male. Aristotle amplifies Plato's brief appendix. "The menstrual fluid is to be classed as prime matter" (29A). Plato's account of the primitives anticipates his student's account of potency and power and actuality, for he says that before the Maker began his work, the Nurse of Becoming was "filled with potencies" (*dynameon*) and that what would become earth, air, fire, and water possessed only "some traces" or "the spoor" (*ichne*) of their own nature (52E, 53B). These traces are the analogues of Plato's *hystera* "wandering" in search of intercourse. The basic triangles, then, with their "irrational" sides, are potencies or capacities to become actual ones.

The Maker (*poietes*), the cause of the generation of the cosmos, takes over a chaos and brings it into "order out of disorder." As we have seen, in the main text, Plato's models are the craftsman and the father. I have suggested that the former is mainly a teaching device and that the latter guides his thought throughout. Analogously, Aristotle uses the Craftsman Model as an auxiliary to Procreation: "The male provides that which fashions [*demiourgoun*] the material" (38B). In the appendix Plato reveals the primitives or letters of his Father Model in the phallus and semen, the former modeling the Maker or the Cause, while the latter models the Forms. Aristotle's account of both male and female is similar. "The male and female principles may be put down first and foremost as origins of generation, the former as containing the efficient cause of generation, the latter, the material of it. . . . But even though we speak of the animal as a whole, as male or female, yet really it is not male or female in virtue of the whole of itself, but only in virtue of a certain faculty and a certain part. . . . Now as a matter of fact such parts are in the female the so-called womb, in the male the testes and penis" (16A). Plato says that the phallus manifests "love for generating" (*gennan eros*) and "love of sexual intercourse" (*sunousias eros*). Yet, at the same time, it symbolizes the generative power of the cosmos, for eros is located not in the loins but in the brain, along with the "divine seed."

Plato's Androgynous Cosmos

Fig. 2.8. The generative power in the world: *Hermes* by Alcamenes, Pergamom, fifth century B.C., Archaeological Museum, Istanbul: *Timaeus* 73CD, 91B

This symbolic value of the phallus in the *Timaeus* is represented by the strange statue of Hermes: "A squared pillar having just a head at the top and the phallus erect in the middle. . . . The generative power was thought to be in the head and to be the psyche. Hermes was the generative power in the world at large, as it were, the universal fertilizing psyche . . . worshipped in the form of an erect phallus."[14] The *Timaeus*, in the midst of all its geometry, shows the importance of love in Plato's system.[15] At the start (22C) we learn that it is *philia* that constitutes the cement of the universe. At the end we learn that it is *eros* that constitutes its generative power.

The mystery of the relation of the Forms to this world stays with us in the *Timaeus*. On pages 50–52 Plato says that the Forms "do not enter into anything else anywhere," that Space or the Receptacle is "entirely distinct from the Forms entering it," that "it does not in any way take on any character like the things that enter it; . . . and yet, in some perplexing and most baffling way, it partakes of the intelligible." As for phenomena, they are not a part of the Receptacle, though they cannot exist apart from it, and in some fashion they "copy the eternal things." It would have been obvious to his students that Plato was taking sides on a much debated issue in biology: the roles of the female and male in generation. Does each contribute seed to conception, or only the male? He adopts the view of Anaxagoras, described by Aristotle: "The semen comes from the male, while the female provides space for it" (63B). Although immaterial, the *pneuma* or *spiritus* in the semen carries the Form, enabling the child to copy its father. This provides the first part of the biological basis for the mysterious ways in which the phenomenal world "copies" the Forms and the Receptacle "captures a part of" them.

The remaining part is suggested by his account of the two triangles introduced a page later (53D). Why does Plato choose only two primitives? why does he choose two triangles? Why, from the multitude of triangles, does he choose the half-square and the half-equilateral? Why not, for the job of constructing the regular solids, choose one whole triangle, the equilateral, and one whole square, as his student Theaetetus had just done, and Euclid, his student-once-removed at the Academy, was about to do in Book XIII of the *Elements?* Why, instead, does he cut their primitives in half, as it were? The answers are not obvious. Perhaps several factors motivated his choice of primitives. One was his love of economy. Another was his desire to fit together the latest findings of the various sciences. Another was his desire to render harmless the discovery of the irrational numbers, so disturbing to the classical order. He says: "All triangles derive their origin from these two triangles," that is, triangles containing the sides $\sqrt{2}$ and $\sqrt{3}$ (53D). This geometrical statement suggests in his arithmetic its analogue, which he does not state, that all irrational numbers are expressible as sums or multiples of $\sqrt{2}$ and $\sqrt{3}$. These irrationals are to be made innocuous by deriving whole numbers from them. Moreover, by finding a place for them in the foundations of his system of the world, Plato can fit

Plato's Androgynous Cosmos 37

mathematics with physics. But Plato has motives even more relevant than this. He wants to construct a "cosmos" (meaning order and harmony) in which all parts fit, not just at the beginning, but also at the end.

Obviously, Plato's choice of primitives is determined by the system he purposes to construct, his immediate purpose being to construct four of the regular solids, leaving the fifth, the dodecahedron, present but unconstructed. This enables him, unlike Theaetetus and Euclid, to limit himself to two primitives. The diagram (fig. 2.2) shows that one triangle "generates" three of the regular solids: the pyramid, the octahedron, and the icosahedron; the other "generating" the fourth, the cube. Most intricate geometrically is the third, which, along with the fifth, is eulogized by Herman Weyl as "certainly one of the most beautiful and singular discoveries made in the whole history of mathematics."[16] While Euclid the geometer was to conclude his *Elements* with the construction of the regular solids (perhaps the chief goal of his deductive geometry), Plato the physicist tries to incorporate these geometrical entities in a physical system by interpreting them as "primary bodies" to make fire, air, water, and earth, the four "elements" of Empedocles.

But now, Plato the biologist uses this physical system as a model for the human body. The diagram (fig. 2.2) shows that the parts of the model (the macrocosm) find their miniature counterparts in the thing modeled (the microcosm) the account of which, if I am right, is the final cause or purpose of the whole project. The nature of this final cause should have no slight or trivial influence on Plato's choice of primitives. As one expects, and as the diagram shows, part of the macrocosm generated by one triangle has its counterpart in the chest containing the heart and lungs, the other part, generated by the second triangle, in the upper belly housing the stomach and liver. Plato says that "a division is built within the cavity of the breast—or 'thorax,' as it is called— as if to fence off two separate apartments, one for men, the other for women, by placing the midriff between them" (69E). Although amused, we find it elsewhere confirmed that Plato views the human being as androgynous, and correspondingly, so is the cosmos. Aristotle notes that "in cosmology they speak of the Earth as female and call it 'mother,' while they give to the heaven and the sun the title 'father' . . . " (16A). But the diagram does not show and Plato does not hint until he writes the appendix that the two triangles, the primitives of his physics, have their counterparts in his biology. Once again, it would have been obvious to his students at the Academy that Plato was adopting the remaining part of Anaxagoras's view on sex-differentiation and meshing it with his physics. Aristotle records it: "Anaxagoras and certain other physiologers say that this antithesis exists right back in the semen . . . and that the male comes from the right testis, the female from the left . . . "(63B). This view, that there are two elements in the semen that determine the sex of the child, would have seemed to Plato just as plausible as his own view that two elementary triangles determine the nature of the physical world and just as plausible as the "discoveries" of the liver as the seat of divination and the lungs as the refrigerators of the heart—all "discoveries" that he accepted. Doubtless Plato would have seen that his adoption of the view that the semen contains two elements would preserve the symmetry between his systems of biology and physics. It may have influenced him in his physics to choose two entities of the same sort, specifically, two triangles, instead of one triangle and one square, and then to construct two corresponding parts within the mortal part of the cosmos.

The metaphors construction and creation point to different aspects of the Forms. Construction, which highlights the composite Form, the plan or pattern needed by the Demiurge to make a cosmos, subsequently captured the imaginations of physicists and most readers. This feature is absent from the creation metaphor in which a father creates a child without working from a plan. The latter highlights the basic Forms, the chromosomes (as it were) of the cosmos, and has no need even for

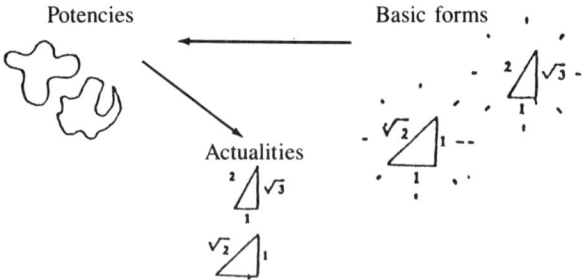

Fig. 2.9. The chromosomes of the cosmos: *Timaeus* 52E–55C

intermediate Forms, a Form for each object in the actual world: The basic triangles "ceased acting" when they had "generated" the regular solids (55B). Thus is eliminated the need for a vast number of unnecessary Forms in the Platonic heaven with which Plato, at this stage in his thinking, was trying to dispense. The basic Forms, that is, the basic triangles *from which* actual triangles are "copied," are distinct from actual triangles just as the *pneuma* or spirit of semen is "no part of the resulting embryo," or as Euclid's triangles are distinct from actual triangles, the things we draw and erase. They are distinct also from those other potential triangles *out of which* the latter are made: the "traces" or matter, or the chalk, as well as from the Receptacle or space *in which* the actualities appear.

Finally, Plato was taking sides on yet another issue in biology relevant to the nature of the cosmos. This was the question of preformation versus epigenesis. At conception, as Plato notes in the appendix, the entities "sown upon the womb" are "unformed" (*adiaplasta*). This suggests that there is no homunculus or animalcule in the womb and that Plato rejected preformationism before Aristotle did, a suggestion confirmed by Plato's account of the "conception" of the cosmos in Part II. The diagram (fig. 2.2) shows that there would be no little cosmos in the Receptacle at "conception," only little triangles.

The cosmos, then, is this phenomenal world seen as either a work of art constructed by the Demiurge from a plan or an offspring generated through the intercourse of a father and a mother. These root ideas of Western thought undergo so little transformation through the ages that one finds them recurring in a mixed metaphor as a fundamental assumption of modern physics: Physical phenomena consist always of the interaction of energy with matter. But the anthropomorphic features have been merely submerged. The word "energy" (in work), which has the same root as "demiurge," was coined by Aristotle, doubtless with the idea of craftsmanship in mind; the concept of "matter" is rooted, as we have seen, in the idea of the essential contribution of the female in generation; while the idea of "interaction" between energy and matter to produce the phenomenal world probably derives from the idea of intercourse between male and female. "We have, so to speak," as Einstein says in an analogous context, "forgotten what features in the world of experience caused us to frame these concepts, and we have great difficulty in representing the world . . . without the [old] spectacles."[17]

UNITY OF THE TIMAEUS

The hypothesis I proposed at the outset, that in the appendix to the *Timaeus* Plato discloses a main guiding idea or root metaphor of that work, I now consider to be established. I have shown that the idea of procreation must be ranked alongside the idea of craftsmanship as a dominant influence in Plato's thought. Moreover, I have shown that although the Craftsman Model with its built-in geometry may be Plato's main teaching device, relative to his theory it contains grave omissions, which the Procreation Model, exhibiting Plato's trinity of the mother, the child, and the father, is able to fill. Finally, by appealing to the "primitives" of this model, specified in the appendix, certain dark areas in Plato's theory can be clarified. The symmetry of the dual features of the male and female sex organs (begetting and forming, and cradling and nourishing, respectively) is preserved in the corresponding features of the finished theory. Thus the "obscure and baffling" Receptacle and Nurse of the phenomenal world combines in herself the dual role of dry nurse and wet nurse: She is both Space and Matter. Similarly, the Maker and Father of this universe, so "difficult to discover," is both the Cause of generation and the Model Form: "the source wherefrom (*hothen*) the phenomenal world is copied and begotten" (50CD). Such an interpretation accords with the controversial reading of the last sentence of the *Timaeus* in which the cosmos is described as "the image of its maker" (*eikon tou poietou*).[18] The Maker of the *Timaeus* shares this dual role with the Good of the *Republic*. As a father (*pater*) who generates offspring in his likeness, the Good is both a cause (*aitia*) and a form (*idea*) (506E–509E).

If my hypothesis is accepted, then the last part of the *Timaeus* cannot properly be called an appendix. Plato's account of sex becomes an integral part of the book. Like some other composers of long poems that otherwise might remain puzzling mysteries, Plato at the end provides a key to the parable of the *Timaeus*.[19] This brings me to the other apparent irrelevancy in the work, which has puzzled some readers: the lengthy introductory summary of the Ideal State, its actualization in ancient Athens, and the latter's defeat of Atlantis. If the *Republic* and the *Timaeus* are complementary works on the same primary subject, one would expect Plato to consider them together—and he does this. Before starting- "today's" lecture on man as a microcosm, he recapitulates, for the benefit of his students in the Academy, some salient points in "yesterday's" lecture on man as a micropolis. One salient point concerns the ordering of sexual unions (18E) and the rejection of "disorder [*ataktos*] and promiscuity" (*Republic* 458D). This is a harbinger of things to come in "today's" lecture, for it models the second or auxiliary causes that, "devoid of intelligence, produce their effects at random and without order" (*atakton*) (46E). Moreover, in the account of ancient Athens, we learn that "much attention was devoted to the cosmic order, deriving from those divine principles all arts applied to human life down to divination and the art of medicine which aims at health" (24C). This anticipates, if I am right, the primary subject of the *Timaeus*. Finally, we learn that the greatest achievement of ancient Athens lay in the fact that she overcame the invaders from Atlantis who sought to gain "absolute sway" (25B–C.cf. 91C). This triumph of an "orderly and regular system" (24C) over an unruly power is a prelude to the central cosmogonical idea of the *Timaeus* in which "Intelligence overruled Necessity" (48A). Thus both the beginning and the end of the *Timaeus*, which appear to be irrelevant appendages, are properly seen to fit into the body of the work. The *Timaeus* is a finished work of art.

CONCLUSION:
PROCREATION AS A MODEL FOR THE MIND

In our search for the origins of mind and the origins of the substance-attribute theory, we have made some progress. In Plato's Procreation Model we found at the first level the trinity of mother, father, and child, and, when spelled out, the womb as receptacle and as nourishment; the phallus and semen; and the offspring. These lend themselves well to a theory of mind with the notions of passivity and activity and of an understanding and a will, with thoughts and images as products of intercourse between the two sets. They lend themselves also to making the conceptions of substance-attribute and substance-inherence. But we notice that Plato says little about the mind and nothing about substance-attribute theories in this book.

Now that we have seen how Plato applies the main associated commonplaces of the Procreation Model to exhibit part of the structure and operations of the cosmos, we can discern how these same features of the model may be applied to something much smaller, namely, the structure and operations of the human mind. The "large letters" of the macrocosm will help us to read the same letters in the microcosm. Plato's trinity of mother, father, and child should reappear in subsequent philosophies of mind. One expects it to reappear most vividly within the next generation in the theory of mind devised by Plato's great student Aristotle.

CHAPTER 3

Using the Metaphor:
Aristotle's Androgynous Mind

Linnaeus and Couvier have been my two Gods, though in very different ways, but they were mere schoolboys to old Aristotle.

Charles Darwin

In this chapter I reveal the fecundity of the Procreation Model as a design for the structure and operations of the mind, with special attention to the active mind, its distinction from passive mind, and the operation of perception. In order to do this I exhibit aspects of Aristotle's theory in his *De Anima* from the standpoint of Plato's Procreation Model as modified by Aristotle in *Generation of Animals*. We see also the beginning of the subject-predicate and substance-attribute models for the mind. In addition I offer an alternative to the dominant contemporary view of Aristotle's theory, according to which the active mind is given little or no functional role. I show that the active mind is of central importance in Aristotle's theory.

PASSIVE AND ACTIVE MINDS

Near the end of the *De Anima* Aristotle formulates, as if concluding the main argument of the book, his famous distinction between the passive and active minds:

> Since just as in the whole of nature there is something that serves as matter for each kind of thing (and this is what is potentially all of them), and something else which is their cause or agent because it makes them all—the two being related as a craft is to its material—so the same distinction must be found in the soul. And thus there is a mind which is what it is because it becomes all things, while there is another which is what it is because it makes all things, like a sort of definite quality such as light; for in a way light makes potential colors into actual colors. And it is this mind which is separable, unaffected, and unmixed, being in essence activity. For that which acts is always superior to that which is acted upon, the originating cause to the matter. . . . Mind is not at one time thinking and at another not. When separated, it is only that which it is essentially, and this alone is immortal and everlasting, but we do not remember because this is not acted upon, whereas the passive mind is perishable and without this thinks nothing (430A 10–25).[1]

Aristotle's Androgynous Mind   43

PROBLEMS AND SOLUTIONS

Owing in large part to the terseness of the style, and probably in part to the garbling of the original edition by later copyists and other handlers, this passage raises several problems of interpretation centering on the vexing problem of active mind or *nous poietikos*. What is the active mind and what is its role? Why does Aristotle say that it survives the death of the body, apparently contradicting his frequently reiterated view that the soul cannot exist apart from the body, just as sight cannot exist apart from the eye? Almost as puzzling is the nature and role of passive mind or *nous pathetikos* and how it differs from the imagination and from the *sensus communis*? How is this mind related to the active mind? Do the two minds interact? Which one does the thinking? Do they have different objects and functions, and are they, therefore, different faculties? Are they things or faculties? Certainly each is named by the noun *nous*, and nouns name things. Perhaps they only appear to be things but in reality are capacities or powers or faculties of things. If the two minds are merely capacities, what is the thing that has these capacities? Is it the body (the heart? the brain?) or the person?

The passage has been much discussed (the last sentence probably more than any other in Aristotle) and given diverse interpretations. These range from the early viewpoint of Alexander of Aphrodisias (fl. A.D. 220), who identified the active mind with God, through the Christian view in the Middle Ages of Aquinas, for whom the active mind was the highest part of the individual soul, to the dominant contemporary view, which considers the active mind to be merely a relic of Aristotle's early student days, "a Platonic wild oat coming home to roost," and of no importance in the overall naturalism of the *De Anima*.[2]

The problems of interpretation raised here are of enormous difficulty. I suggest a new way of looking at these old problems that offers the following solutions: First, the active mind, although it is called "mind," does not think at all; its role is not to think but to activate the passive mind to think. Second, the passive mind does all the thinking, perceiving, imaging, remembering, and recollecting, and it is, or can be, aware of all these activities. Third, both passive and active minds have their place in the heart, the acropolis of the body. Fourth, passive mind, not active mind, "is not at one time thinking and at another not." Fifth, the immortality ascribed to the active mind is the immortality not of any individual or specimen but only of things like it, that is, the species. It is, or amounts to, the immortality of the gene.

THE METAPHORICAL WAY

In order to derive these solutions I place the passage about the two minds in particular and the *De Anima* in general within an obvious but unusual context—obvious because Aristotle doubtless intended it, and unusual because we have forgotten it. It is generally agreed that Aristotle was primarily a biologist.[3] Most commentators even accept the view that the *De Anima* is a biological work,[4] that it was written at about the same time as the *Generation of Animals,* and that the contents overlap; yet they do not sufficiently apply this information in their commentaries. Accordingly, I assume that Aristotle was wearing biological spectacles when he thought out and wrote his psychology, and I assume also that Aristotle was using procreation as a model for his theory of the soul.[5] One of Aristotle's important claims is this: "The soul never thinks without an image" (31A). In my view, the images Aristotle used as he thought about the mind were drawn largely from his experience of the generation of animals. By using this imagery I hope to shed new light on the *De Anima,* especially on the natures and roles of the passive and active minds.

Aristotle begins his account of the two minds with an analogy apparently drawn from his doctrine of the four causes: Passive mind is to active mind as matter is to the efficient cause. This is one of the few occasions in the *De Anima* when the soul or part of it is compared to an efficient cause rather than a formal cause. It is one of the rare occasions on which the mind (*nous*) is referred to as an efficient cause. The passive mind is like matter because it is potentially any kind of thing, while the active mind is the cause of these things because it produces them or makes them actual. Probably because this example is as abstract as the concept of undefined matter, Aristotle provides a more concrete one: The two causes, efficient and material, and thus the two minds, are related as a craft (*techne*) is to its material or, more strictly speaking, as a craftsman is to his materials.

Throughout his writings, Aristotle uses mainly two types of examples or models, one drawn from craftsmanship, the other from biology. The type he uses depends largely on the nature of his primary subject. Thus, he would not use a biological example to illustrate a work in biology. Because the *De Anima* is a biological work, most of the examples come from craftsmanship. Perhaps this explains why Aristotle, even though a biologist, uses as his technical term for matter the word *hyle* (wood), which is part of the primary vocabulary of the Craftsman Model, instead of, as one would expect, a word like our word "matter" (from *meter*, mother), which is part of the primary vocabulary of the Procreation Model.

ARISTOTLE'S PROCREATION MODEL

If Aristotle used the Craftsman Model to teach his students, one wonders what model he used to teach himself.

Although we believe that the *De Anima* is in the middle of a series of six theoretical works in biology that begins with *Parts of Animals* and ends with the *Generation of Animals,* when we read the *De Anima* we think of it as primarily a work in psychology and perception, not biology; and because of our preconceptions, we tend to think of it as a work with geometrical and mechanical rather than biological overtones. Had Aristotle conceived the soul and the mind primarily in craftsmanship terms and used biological illustrations, probably he would have chosen the mother-father relation as his main example. That is, instead of writing: "The two being related as a craft is to its material," he would have written: "The two being related as a father is to a mother."

These two models of craftsmanship and procreation are, as we have seen, also the two main models of Plato's *Timaeus*.[6] Using the Craftsman Model, Plato's main device for teaching his readers how to understand the origin of the cosmos, Plato likens the maker of the cosmos to a craftsman, the materials of the maker to wood, and the cosmos itself to the finished work (cf. *Timaeus* 60: "like wood [*hyle*] waiting for the carpenter"). But when he uses the Procreation Model Plato says, "It is proper to liken the Recipient to the Mother, the Source from which the cosmos is copied and begotten to the Father, and what is engendered between these two to the Offspring" (50D). Since the cosmos and its parts are animals, Plato might have called his own work *Generation of Animals.* As one expects, the main features of procreation that Plato used to work out his cosmogony are present in Aristotle's *Generation of Animals*, written probably about thirty years later than the *Timaeus*. Aristotle uses the same features to work out his own account, not of space and the cosmos within it, but of an entirely different subject matter: the mind and its contents.

Let me abstract some of the main features of Aristotle's Procreation Model from his *Generation of Animals.*

> We may safely set down as the chief principles of generation the male and female factors, the male possessing the efficient cause of generation, the female the material of it . . . (16A). The male provides the form and the principle of movement; the female provides the body, in other words the

material . . . (29A). The male is the active partner (*poietikos*) and does the acting (*poiei*), while the female is the passive partner (*pathetikos*), and is acted upon (*paschei*) . . . (40B, 29A). Since male and female are distinguished by a different faculty and function, and since for the exercise of every function, instruments or organs are needed, then certain parts must exist for the purpose of copulation and procreation . . . for although "male" and "female" are used as epithets for the whole of the animal, it is not male or female in virtue of the whole of itself, but only in virtue of a certain faculty and a certain part. . . . Now as a matter of fact, such parts are in the female what is called the womb, in the male the testicles and penis, so far as all the blooded animals are concerned. . . . Essentially, the male has the power to generate in another while the female generates in itself. . . . In all cases the semen contains within itself that which causes it to be fertile, what is known as the "hot," which is not fire or any similar power but the *pneuma* [or spirit] which is enclosed within the semen or foam-like stuff, and the nature within the *pneuma*, which is the analogue of the element of the stars . . . (36B). The contribution which the female makes is the matter [*hyle*] . . . that out of which it generates . . . and this is in the substance of the menstrual fluid (27B, 20A). The female receives within herself the contribution of both male and female. . . . The embryo is the first mixture of male and female. . . . The development of the embryo takes place in the female (28B, 30B).

Compare here the conception and early life of the kangaroo as described in the February 1979 issue of *National Geographic*: "After fathering the offspring, the dominant male of the group acknowledges no further responsibility. It is the non-liberated mother 'roo who must rear, shelter and feed his progeny." Aristotle names only four "causes"

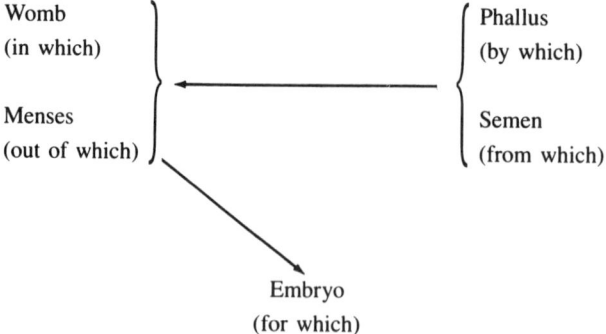

Fig. 3.1. Aristotle's Procreation Model: *GA* 16A, 20A, 28A, 29A, 30B, 36B, 40B

Aristotle's Androgynous Mind   47

(*aitia*). One expects five, the fifth being the Receiving Cause, especially since the Receptacle or its analogue plays a stellar role in Aristotle's account of the soul. Although these features of the Procreation Model are not specified in the *De Anima*, they illuminate in varying degrees Aristotle's accounts of the different faculties of soul, primarily perception and thought, but also nutrition, appetite, and imagination. The method of Aristotle's investigation is indirect: If we seek to define a faculty, we must look not only to its operations or functions (such as thinking and perceiving) but even to its corresponding objects (such as thoughts and percepts) (15A). This method follows Plato's rule of *Republic* (477D): "In a faculty I look only to its objects and its operations [*apergazetai*], and regard these as enough to identify it," a rule Plato went on to apply, a few pages later, to the faculties of perception and thought.

NUTRITION

Aristotle now proceeds to consider the first faculty, that of nutrition. Although he treats this subject with dispatch, he reveals here items that, if supplemented with some from the *Generation of Animals*, shed light on our main problem. The nutritive soul, being shared by all living things, is their primary soul. It is the only soul of plants. Here we have two factors, female and male, the passive and the active, the acting and the being acted upon, as well as the third factor, the offspring. However, although the vocabulary of "female" and "male" is absent from the *De Anima*, it is present in the *Generation of Animals*. There is this dichotomy of female and male, but Aristotle holds that "in plants the female is not separate from the male" (*GA* 41A).

How do the male and female operate within one ensouled body of the plant? Aristotle says that the nutritive faculty of the soul is the same as the reproductive faculty. The one soul has two functions: reproduction and the use of food. The female provides the same material *out of which* the plant is originally formed and is later nourished. The male or primary soul, using heat as its instrument or organ, is the creative cause that causes the material to be (a) set or formed and (b) made digestible. The heat is like the helmsman's hand or the semen (moving and being moved), while the food is like the rudder or the menses (only being moved). If things are defined by their end, the primary soul is that capable of reproducing not the individual specimen but the species. This is the only way the plant can "partake of immortality and divinity" (15B, 16B; *GA* 40B, 41A).

48 Using the Metaphor

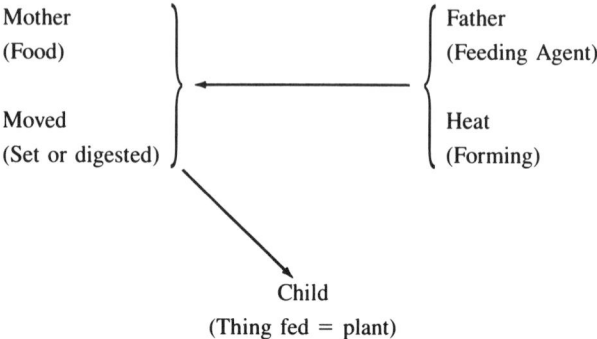

Fig. 3.2. Aristotle's androgynous plant: 15A, 16B, *GA* 40B, 41A

Aristotle's short account of nutrition gives us several hints for solving the problems of active and passive minds: First, the plant is androgynous. Second, the plant has not just two but three aspects: that which is fed, that with which it is fed, and that which feeds (the agent and primary soul). The analogue of this trinity recurs throughout the *De Anima*. Third, two different faculties with different functions merge into one. Fourth, plants can attain immortality but only by carrying on the species.

PERCEPTION

The problem of perception begins for Aristotle or any theorist with the attempt to account for errors in perception, especially illusions. Illusions, as their name suggests, may be thought of as games played against us by a deceiving external world. Without such illusions no theories of perception would have been devised. Illusions persuaded Aristotle and most subsequent scientists to drop certain commonsense beliefs, mainly that perception directly acquaints us with composite material objects. This belief, although appropriate in ordinary cases of perception, meets difficulties with the not-so-extraordinary cases of illusion.

Direct and Indirect Objects

Aristotle's ingenious solution is to distinguish a set of error-free objects of perception intervening between us and the external world. He calls these the objects of perception "strictly speaking" or the "proper objects" (*idia*), because each is the private property of only one sense, that is, "it cannot be sensed by any other sense and in respect of which no error is possible. Thus color is the proper object of sight, sound of

Aristotle's Androgynous Mind 49

hearing, flavor of taste. . . ." (As private properties the objects of perception are distinct from "common objects," the public property of all the senses. These will be considered later.) Presumably these objects are directly perceived because they are the means by which we perceive composite objects such as bells, people, and beacons, which are "indirectly perceived." Notice how well English usage accommodates Aristotle's distinction. We say that we hear sounds as well as bells, see colors as well as beacons, taste flavors as well as cherries, and smell odors as well as bodies. Although the former objects tell us no lies, in perceiving the latter we may make mistakes. For example, "Sight is infallible in its awareness that a certain visual datum is white, although it is perhaps deceived in taking this white datum for a man" (18A, 30B).

The Causal Theory

What is the relevance of the distinction between direct and indirect objects of perception to the problem of passive and active minds? Let us look first at the causal theory on which Aristotle bases his theory of perception: In perceiving we are acted upon; the objects that "can produce [*poietika*] the actuality of perception are external [*exothen*]" to us (17B); the external object does not act directly but only indirectly on us; there is something intervening between us and the external cause that does act directly on us. It is easy to compare this causal theory with the perceptual theory just sketched. The concrete model is found in Aristotle's theory of procreation, with its trinity of mother, father, and child. The mother is interpreted as something being acted upon (*paschei*), the perceiving subject; the father, since he is something creative or productive (*poietikos*) and external (*exothen*) to that which he acts upon, is the external cause and, correspondingly, the indirect or incidental object of perception; the child, the product of the two, or their actuality (*energeia*), is the direct or proper object of perception.

If Aristotle is covertly using the Procreation Model to work out his theory of perception, one hopes that he will make an inadvertent disclosure of its presence in a simple but not so obvious parallel. Fortunately, this hope is realized in the well-known passage about the son of Diares, in which Aristotle gives us one of his very rare examples of an indirect object: "What is meant by the indirect object of sense is as if (*hoion ei*) the whiteness before you were the son of Diares. In which case you perceive Diares, but only indirectly, because Diares is incidental to the whiteness, which you perceive directly. Hence you are not affected by the indirect object itself" (18A, 20–24).

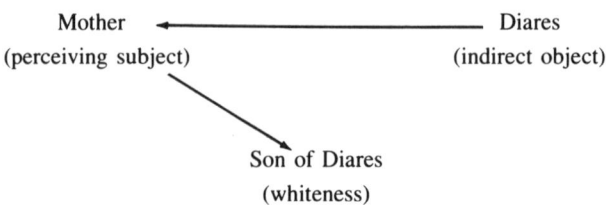

Fig. 3.3. The son of Diares: 18A, 20–24

What you are affected by directly is not Diares, that is, the external object (just as the baseball is acted upon not directly by Babe Ruth but by his bat) but something intervening between you and Diares. This is the analogue of the helmsman's hand, which moves and is moved (16B 25), and of the male semen, which "nature uses as a tool as something that has movement in actuality" (*GA* 30B). Thus, in the perception of an indirect object you are in the situation analogous to that of a mother who, looking at her son before her, tries to identify the father. Even though she may know that "males take after their father more than their mother" (*GA* 67B), she also knows that one can sometimes make a mistake. The translation given above differs from the usual translations in which the son of Diares, not his father, is interpreted as the indirect object.[7] But this is to ignore the phrase "as if," with which, it seems to me, Aristotle introduces an analogy: Just as a son copies his father, so the direct object copies the indirect object, enabling us to perceive the latter indirectly. That the fourth term of the analogy is Diares and not his son is obvious once we assume Aristotle's Procreation Model. Moreover, why should Aristotle choose the cumbersome and intriguing son of Diares as his example for both the direct and indirect objects when Diares himself would serve equally well?[8] Finally, my interpretation is supported by Aristotle's account of the twin activities of act and object, which will be discussed shortly.

Passive and Active Aspects

Ostensibly, Aristotle holds that we are entirely passive in perceiving: perceiving is a being acted upon, a passion, while agency belongs only to the external object that acts upon us. Such a view might seem to be supported by Aristotle's Procreation Model, specifically by his strange view (strange from our late twentieth-century standpoint) that in procreation the female is entirely passive. But to ascribe such a view to Aristotle is to ignore the role of the active male element in procreation.

Aristotle's Androgynous Mind 51

Taken as a whole, procreation is both active and passive. Aristotle should therefore hold that in perception we are both active and passive. That he does hold this view is confirmed by his remarks about direct and indirect perception: Seeing colors or hearing sounds is free from error; in such so-called acts of perception we are passive, but in perceiving colored or sounding objects, or in "taking this white datum for a man," we can run into error. There must therefore be within us a principle that enables us to combine or synthesize the sense data so that we can make a wrong perception, "for falsehood always involves a synthesis" (*synthesei*), while "the principle which makes [*poioun*] the synthesis is in every case the mind" (18A, 30B). Accordingly, while we passively receive sense data, we (or our minds) actively perceive composite external objects.

Act and Object

There is more than one type of product of the external object and the perceiving subject. Aristotle distinguishes two activities or operations: the "activity" of perceiving and the object. We distinguish, for example, between feeling a toothache and the toothache, or between seeing a color and the color. Nevertheless, in this century G. E. Moore, in his famous article "The Refutation of Idealism," felt the need to defend this distinction against its contrary: "To identify 'blue' or any other of what I have called 'objects' of sensation with the corresponding sensation is in every case a self-contradictory error."[9] Bertrand Russell, in an equally famous work, *The Problems of Philosophy,* also defended it: "This question of the distinction between act and object in our apprehending of things is vitally important, since our whole power of acquiring knowledge is bound up with it."[10] While Moore and Russell held that in the act of sensing data such as colors and sounds we are active, Aristotle holds that the so-called act is a passive receiving.

Aristotle's distinction is a simple application of his views on the generation of animals. But Plato in his "Secret Doctrine" of perception, which he presents in *Theaetetus* 156–57, shows this application better than Aristotle: "There is nothing but motion, of which there are two kinds: one, an active power [*dynamin . . . poiein*], the other passive [*dynamin . . . paschein*]. From the intercourse and friction of these two kinds of motion with their corresponding faculties, one of acting, the other of being acted upon . . . arise offspring, endless in number but in pairs of twins." One twin is always the act of sensing (for example, seeing, hearing, smelling); the other is the sense datum or sensum (for example, a color, a sound, a smell, etc.). "As soon as, say, an eye and an appropriate object come within range, they beget whiteness and the corresponding seeing . . . the eye becomes a seeing eye and the object becomes a white thing." "The conclusion is that nothing is one thing just by itself, but is always in process of becoming [*gignesthai*] in relation to something. . . . We should speak of things as 'being born' [*gignomena*], and 'being created' [*poioumena*]." In my view, this "secret doctrine" is Plato's own. The use of procreation as a model for perception harks back to the Procreation Model of the *Timaeus*.

Although in his psychology he discards Plato's sexual vocabulary of "intercourse," "parents," "birth," and "twins," Aristotle's account of perception has much the same structure. There are significant differences which may be due to Aristotle's more reactionary views on sex.

Let us start with the "pairs of twins." The twins are not identical; one is female, the other male. These model the operations or functions (*energeia*) of the perceiving subject and external object, respectively. The first twin is female because she is a passive affection (*pathos*), a daughter, as it were, of the perceiving subject. The second twin is male because he is an active operation or production (*poiesis*), a son, as it were, of the external object, like the son of Diares. Aristotle uses audition as his main example: "The actuality of that which can hear is hearing or listening, while the activity of the object producing sound is sound or sonance" (20A 7–8).[11] The same is true of all other senses and sensible objects. These two are counterparts of what philosophers nowadays call "the act" and "the object," or "the sensation" and "the sense datum" or "sensum." But while the two can be distinguished, as actualities the object and the sensation are "one and the same" and therefore cannot be abstracted from each other: "When that which can hear is actually hearing, and when that which can sound is sounding,

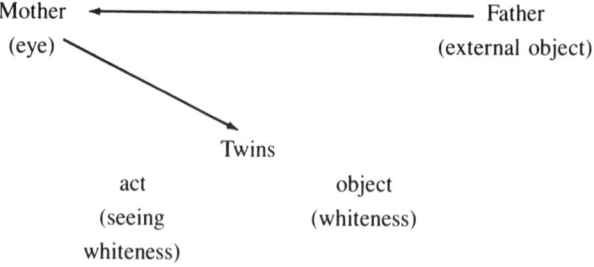

Fig. 3.4. Plato's twins: *Theaetetus* 156–7

Aristotle's Androgynous Mind   53

then the actual hearing and the actual sound are merged in one" (25B 30–31). Moore and Russell departed from Aristotle's view, but Russell, within the decade, turned-about and adopted a position close to the present one: "The possibility of distinguishing the sensation from the sense datum vanishes. . . . Accordingly, the sensation that we have when we see a patch of color simply is that patch of color. . . ."[12] The twins of Plato and Aristotle, however, are not modeled upon ordinary twins. It is likely that they are modeled upon the first contributions of the male and female in procreation, for it is easy to see that the merger of the sensation and the sense datum is modeled upon the embryo, "the first compound [*proton migma*] of male and female" (*GA* 28B 34–35).

From their different views of procreation, especially of the role of the female, one can understand a significant difference between the views of Plato and Aristotle on perception. The former, followed by Galen and Roger Bacon, subscribes to the Emission or Emanation theory, in which visual rays emanate from the eye to clothe the object. The latter, followed by the great Arab optical theorist Ibn al Haitham and Kepler and his modern followers, subscribes to the Immission theory in which visual species or, eventually, rays of light, enter the eye.

What is the relevance to his account of mind of Aristotle's initial distinction between the sensation and the sense datum and then of the eventual merging of this pair? The answer, I believe, is that it models the merging of an analogous pair: the thinking and the thought. As we have seen, both unions are illustrated by the first merger of the female and male contributions in generation.

"In the Mind"

How are these twin activities, the act of sensing and the sensum, related to the perceiving subject? Aristotle's answer, now so familiar to us, is that they are both in the subject: "Just as acting (*poiesis*) and the being acted upon (*pathesis*) are in that which is acted upon (*paschonti*) and not in the agent (*poiounti*) so also the activity (*energeia*) of the perceived object and the act of the sensing subject lie in the latter" (26A 10ff).

This simple answer is of great importance, for with it, we are probably close to the origin of that notorious concept in the history of philosophy: "in the mind." Aristotle defines the phrase "in a subject" on the first page of his *Categories*: "By in a subject I mean what is in something not as a part but which cannot exist apart from what it is in."

In Aristotle's thinking what is in a subject is not related to the subject as peas in a saucepan are not related to the saucepan in which they are cooking. The relation, rather, is that peculiar relation between the qualities in the Receptacle and the Receptacle itself of Plato's *Timaeus.* Such qualities "cling to existence on pain of being nothing at all" and yet are "entirely distinct from" the Receptacle (50–52). It is likely that Plato derived this concept from the image of the embryo in the womb, for he likens the Receptacle and its contents to a mother and child. Just as likely, Aristotle the geneticist and student of the *Timaeus* used the same imagery, for he tells us that "the female receives within herself the contribution of both male and female" (*GA* 28B). These twin activities, as we have seen, merge in one activity, the perceived object (for example, whiteness). Accordingly, just as the embryo cannot exist apart from the womb, so such sensa as whiteness, sweetness, etc., must be in a perceiving subject; that is, they cannot exist apart from it although they are not a part of it.

The Perceiving Subject

What, then, is the perceiving subject? Is it any one of the senses or sense organs, or is it something prior, such as the common sense or its organ? On the face of it Aristotle holds the former view. Each sense perceives not only its own proper objects, but also proper objects of the other senses, common incidental objects, and, lastly, remote incidental objects. It is likely, however, that Aristotle does not reveal his entire theory in the *De Anima,* for he gives hints of a more satisfactory solution. He refers to an "ultimate sense organ" and to "a common faculty of sense which apprehends the common sensibles directly," and he claims: "That which asserts the difference between sweet and white must be one faculty . . . which thinks and perceives" (*noei kai ais thanetai*) (25A, 26B). These hints are developed in the short treatises that follow the *De Anima* and comprise the *Parva Naturalia.*[13] The former can be modified in the light of the latter to make a more plausible theory.

If this is done we find there is one ultimate faculty of sense (*aisthetikon panton*). Aristotle argues by analogy: "Just as white and sweet and many different qualities may be together in numerically one substance," so for "all sense objects . . . we must suppose numerically one faculty of sense" (*On Sense,* 49A). This important passage probably marks one of the early attempts to envisage what we call "mind." Clearly, this one faculty of sense apprehends directly both the proper objects and the common sensibles and is otherwise called the common sense (*koine aisthesis*) or the primary sense faculty (*proton aisthetikon*)

(*On Memory*, 50A). Correspondingly, there is "one master sense organ" where the primary sense faculty is seated. In all sanguineous animals this is the common sensorium (*koinon aistheterion*) of all the sense organs and lies in the heart (*On Sleep*, 56A); *On Youth*, 69A).

Once we accept one common sense for all directly perceived objects, we can remove a difficulty regarding the common sensibles. Aristotle distinguishes between the special objects (for example, color, smell, taste, and sound) and the common sensibles (for example, movement, rest, figure, size, number, and unity). Moreover, he says that we perceive the latter "by each sense incidentally" (25A). This distinction led to a very different distinction that is still widely accepted. Later theorists thought that colors, smells, etc., were in us, and that size, shape, etc., were in the external object. Thus a perceptual distinction was taken for an ontological one. Hence arose the distinction between primary and secondary qualities. But since both common objects and proper objects are directly perceived, they exist in the primary sense faculty, and no ontological difference can be inferred.

With the help of the Procreation Model, we can answer another question about the perceiving subject, which "is potentially such as the object of perception is when actualized" (*entelechia*) (18A). What exactly is it that becomes the object? Is it the sense organ, that is, what I now regard as the common sensorium, or is it the primary sense faculty? We saw earlier that the female has two roles to play in procreating. She provides the receptacle and the matter, or the menses, which become the embryo. That is, the potential embryo is actualized by the male. By analogy, it is not the sensorium but the sense faculty that is potentially the percept. That is, the percept is a capacity to become an actuality, just as the menses are a capacity to become the embryo.

Aristotle sums up his account of perception: "The sense is that which is receptive [*dektikon*] of the form of sensible objects without the matter," and "The primary sense organ is that in which such a potency resides" (24A). This raises two questions. First, we must ask once more: What is the perceiving subject? Is it part of the body or is it the capacity of that body? Although Aristotle vacillates, there is little doubt about his real view, apparently belied by his example: The sense receives the form just as "wax receives the impression of the signet ring without the iron or gold" (24A). Wax is a material entity whose material shape is altered. But Aristotle does not intend these words to be taken in their gross original sense. He is using a material example to express an immaterial concept, just as Plato used the sun to illustrate the Good. Thus, although partially hidden, the real perceiving subject of the *De Anima* is neither the senses or sense organs nor the common sensorium. But it is the *sensus communis*. Percepts are in this subject just as the qualities are in Plato's Receptacle or, to go farther back, as the embryo is in the womb.

Second, how are the immaterial forms transmitted and received? Aristotle's model of the signet ring and the impression on wax is useful for teaching his students. But since the *De Anima* is a biological work, what model does Aristotle use to teach himself? Probably the image in his mind is the male in procreation. Nothing material comes from the male and yet the semen is material. Within it, however, is the *pneuma* or *elan vital* containing the principle of form that enables the child to copy its parent.

Aristotle supplements this image with that of fig juice curdling milk. Nothing material comes from it: "It does not remain as part of the bulk which is set and curdled; and the same applies to the semen" (*GA* 37A). There is an analogy between the *pneuma* of procreation and the *aether* of causation and hence of perception: "*Pneuma* [or spirit] is analogous to the element of the stars." This element is aether or the quintessence, which is immortal and divine and is also the medium in vision. It is called in the *De Anima* "the diaphanous," and it intervenes between the external object and the eye. *Pneuma* belongs to the "everlasting upper cosmos," and light is its actuality (18B).

We know a little about light today. Aristotle knew less, but without telescopes or other technological devices, he reached a view startlingly like ours. He did so not just by drawing a simple parallel with procreation, but also combining his biological knowledge with a commonsense rejection of action at a distance, such as in the relation between the sun and the earth.

IMAGINATION AND WILLING

Aristotle only sketches an account of imagination, but this sketch helps us bridge the gap between perception and thought. Presiding over the *De Anima* is the Aristotelian trinity of the mother, the father, and the child. In elementary perception this trinity is interpreted as the perceiving subject, the external object, and the percept, respectively. In the case of imagination Aristotle keeps the same mother but changes the father to produce out of the same "material" a new child. The new father is no longer the external object but a power within us. We can excite images at pleasure and make our own scenery as we see fit. This making (*poiesasthai*) of images (*phantasia*) lies in our power whenever we will (*boulom-*

Aristotle's Androgynous Mind   57

etha) (27B). Such images are the new children of the same mother. But whatever power we have over our own images, perceptions are not dependent on our willing. They are the products of the external object and myself as the perceiving subject, although, as we have seen, in the perception of a composite external object we, or our minds, are both passive and active. What of the mother? Does she remain the same? We have to turn to the sequel of the *De Anima* for the answer.

In the little book *On Memory and Recollection* we learn that she does remain the same, for "the image is an affection [*pathos*] of the primary sense faculty" (50A). Thus, our actual images as well as our perceptions are affections of the same faculty. Perception and imagination are merged in one just as "the nutritive faculty of soul is the same as the reproductive" (16A). Thus, in perception and imagination, to use again the vocabulary of the model, the mother remains the same. In the same book we learn, moreover, that not only our knowledge of time but also memory and recollection belong to this same faculty (50A, 51A). Finally, in the book *On Sleep* we find not only that with the *sensus communis* do we make judgments but also that this is the faculty "whereby one is conscious that one sees and hears" (55A). The realm of such consciousness is expanded in the *Nicomachean Ethics* to embrace thinking as well as perceiving: "If we perceive, then we perceive that we perceive, and if we think, [then we perceive] that we think" (1170A). Thus in Aristotle's view the common-sense faculty turns out to be a most comprehensive one. It includes not only perception, but also imagination, memory, recollection, judgment, cognition of time, and, above all, consciousness of perception and thought.

We have seen that the organ for this central receptive or passive faculty is the *common sensorium* located in the heart. As one expects, the heart also is the master organ for the central active faculty paralleling the receptive one. In the *Movements of Animals* (703A) we learn that desire is the "central origin" or cause of motion. Corresponding to it is a bodily substance, connate pneuma, that "moves and is moved." "All animals possess it and exercise their strength in virtue of it." But this is only a medium or instrument used by an immaterial agent that moves without being moved, namely, the soul in its willing or causal aspect. The medium is located in the heart, which is also the place of the soul as ruler of the whole animal. Just as a well-governed polis is ruled from a central place, so the animal "has no need of soul in each part" but is ruled by one soul situated in "a central origin of authority" over the body.

PASSIVE AND ACTIVE MINDS REVISITED

On first view, Aristotle's accounts of nutrition, perception, and imagination seemed to be accounts only of passive faculties. But in each case we found partially hidden along with the passive capacity, the corresponding active power. We expect the same to be true of the faculty of thought, specifically, that there is an active power corresponding to it. When we come to the passage near the end of the book about the two minds (with which I began this chapter), we see that there is a corresponding active power, but for the first time, Aristotle clearly shows the passive and the active principles alongside each other. Let me translate most of the passage from *De Anima* (430A) into the language of the Procreation Model. For the word "mind" in its two senses I substitute the more general words "passive potency" and "active power."

> Since just as in the whole of life there is the mother that provides the material for the offspring (which material becomes the offspring), while on the other hand there is the father that is their cause and is creative by creating these offspring . . . so the same distinction must be found in the soul. And there is a passive capacity, which is what it is because it becomes all its objects, while there is another active power, which is what it is because it makes all its objects, for in a way *pneuma* is the instrument for making potential offspring into actual ones. And it is this active power that is separable, unaffected, and unmixed, being in essence agency. For the active male is always superior to the passive female, the creative cause to the matter.

In the light of the material covered in this chapter we see that this passage could have served as a helpful introduction to the *De Anima,* for the dichotomy of passive and active is, I believe, a major theme of the book. Except, perhaps, for the adjectives "separable" and "unmixed," and the phrase "all things," for which I have substituted "all its objects," the passage fits nutrition, perception, and imagination, as well as thought. Thus Aristotle's book *On the Soul* might have been called *On the Androgynous Soul.*

PASSIVE MIND

We saw earlier that Aristotle argues by analogy in order to derive one ultimate perceiving subject: Just as many different qualities may be in one physical substance, so "we must suppose numerically one faculty of sense" that apprehends these many qualities (*On Sense 49A*). It seems likely that Aristotle merely extended the analogy in order to reach his

Aristotle's Androgynous Mind

view that this ultimate faculty of sense is more than a sense faculty, for we found that the latter was expanded to embrace the many different faculties of perception, imagination, memory, self-awareness, etc. Since this faculty is so comprehensive, I can drop the cumbersome title "common-sense faculty" and adopt the name it deserves: "the mind." In my view, this mind is identical with Aristotle's passive mind, the puzzling *nous pathetikos* of the *De Anima,* and different from the active mind yet to be discussed. This mind is the "mother" who remains unchanged in the passage from perception through imagination to thought.

As one expects, the passive mind provides the place for the materials of thought. These materials are memories and recollections stored in the receptacle of the mind as analogous entities are in the womb. They are actualized as images. One might ask How are memories like menses? and answer Both are merely potencies to become images or embryos. They must be activated by our own willing and by the father, respectively. "For the thinking soul, images take the place of direct perceptions" (31A). Moreover, of the two minds, the passive mind is the one with self-awareness or consciousness of thinking, imaging, perceiving, or remembering. Finally, just as "the female receives within herself the contributions of both male and female" (*GA* 28B), and just as only the mother carries the embryo, so only the passive mind can conceive and carry a thought. That is, only the passive mind can think. Aristotle confirms this when he says that the mind is "receptive" (*dektikon*) and that "thinking is a form of being acted upon" (*paschein*) (29A, 29B).

What are the objects of thought? Presumably they are, among other objects, the same as the objects of knowledge: "Knowledge is of universals, and these are somehow in the soul itself" (17B); that is, universals, such as man and animal, as opposed to particulars, such as this man Callias, are somehow in the passive mind. But Aristotle repeatedly claims that the soul never thinks without an image. He says also that "the thinking faculty thinks the forms in mental *images*" (31B). It seems likely to me that Aristotle subscribes to a symbolist theory of thinking, according to which universals are in the mind only in the sense that particular images are in the mind or particular diagrams or symbols are before it—particular entities that represent things beyond themselves. He adopts, then, a position similar to that of the mathematicians in the Divided Line of Plato's *Republic* (509f), who think *with* diagrams but *of* the Forms. "It is impossible even to think without an image. The same affection (*pathos*) is involved in thinking as in using a diagram . . . the man who is thinking, although he may not be thinking of a finite size, still puts a finite size before his eyes'' (*On Memory* 49B–50A). Just as there are two sorts of objects of mathematics, so there are two of thought: the image and the universal. The precise nature of the latter need not concern us here.

ACTIVE MIND

Before considering how the mind, that is, passive mind, becomes its objects, and whether it is perishable, let us consider the nature of active mind or *nous poietikos*, and let us see whether it is identical to any central active power we have already met; in other words, let us see whether it parallels *nous pathetikos*. Aristotle appears to discuss it almost without intermission in the last half of the passage about the passive and active minds quoted on the first page of this chapter. Most of the remarks can be readily interpreted in the light of the Procreation Model so that it becomes a fitting mate for its passive counterpart, a father to marry the mother as it were, and without any mysterious residues. Some of the remarks, however, while tame and obvious in the language of the model, are paradoxical in the language of the theory.

Some earlier commentators, such as Alexander of Aphrodisias in the second century and Zabarella in the sixteenth (perhaps because of such remarks as: "it makes all things," "such as light," and "being in essence activity"), identified the active mind with God, the passive mind being illuminated by the cosmic mind.[14] Such a view seems improbable, since Aristotle tells us earlier in the passage that the distinction between the two minds, and therefore the active mind itself, "must be found in the soul."

If the active mind is not identical with an external God but exists in every human being, what is its nature and function in the soul? Recent commentators typically hold that the active mind thinks and, presumably, that its essence is thinking.[15] Such a view is held perhaps because Aristotle calls the active mind *nous*, variously translated as "mind," "intellect," or "reason," and because the active mind is "in essence activity." This view is reinforced by the sentence "Mind is not at one time thinking and at another not," appearing in the middle of Aristotle's remarks about active mind in the last half of the passage. The view that the active mind thinks is, I believe, mistaken.

To start with, it is likely that the sentence "Mind is not at one time thinking . . . " is out of its proper place. Here it interrupts the course of the thought. In this I accept the decision of W. D. Ross to remove it, not necessarily to another chapter as he does, but at least from this part of the passage.[16] In my view, Aristotle's remark deals with passive mind. We have seen that thinking or having thoughts occurs in the mind and is a passive affection (29A–30A).

The phrase "in essence activity" (*te ousia on energeia*) may be taken in either of two senses that amount to the same meaning: (1) as "in essence agency," because Aristotle's invention *energeia*, which has the same root as Plato's *demiourgos* (*ergon, work*), refers to activity as opposed to passivity, agency as contrasted with being acted upon; or (2) as the actuality of the active mind as opposed to its potency or power, that is, making or creating. Moreover, if the active mind is likened to a *hexis* such as light ("Between the doer and the deed there is the doing," *hexis* [*Metaphysics* 1022B]), or if it is modeled upon the father, then, in either case, its essence is making or creating thoughts rather than having them. Thus we have the paradoxical view that a thing called "active mind" does not think at all. The paradox vanishes, however, if we accept that the role of *nous poietikos* (an expression that does not occur here, although its use is justified) is not to think but to activate the passive mind to think.

If I am right, it is likely that the active mind is the same agency we found operating as the active power corresponding to the passive faculties in perception and imagination, particularly because it is unlikely that Aristotle posits three creative causes, one for each passive faculty. Once more, the one agency for many faculties is an extension of his argument from analogy. This power parallels the passive faculty of thought, which only some animals possess. In the *Posterior Analytics* we learn that although all animals possess sense perception, only in some does the sense impression persist. Of the latter, only some have the power to combine many impressions into a memory. Of the last group, in turn, only some can combine many memories into a single experience, that is, possess the faculty of thought (99B–100A). But this is also to possess the power to act, for the power of combining the many into one belongs to the active mind. If this is so, what is Aristotle's biological account of the difference between human and other animals?

This brings me to the difficult last sentence of the passage, which begins: "When separated, it is only that which it is essentially, and this alone is immortal and everlasting. . . ." As we have just noticed, Aristotle in the *De Anima* compares the active mind to light. But elsewhere he tells us that its vehicle is *pneuma*, which is analogous to aether, whose actuality is light. In the *Generation of Animals* he tries to answer "a very great puzzle": "When and how does mind arise in those who have it, and where does it come from?" Aristotle's partial answer is that mind enters into the semen of the male "from outside" (*thyrathen*), that it is "divine," and that the semen is the vehicle for *pneuma*, which, in turn, "is accompanied by the portion of soul-principle, the so-called *nous*." Aristotle, it seems to me, is here anticipating the discovery of the gene. This is "separate from physical matter" (36B, 37A). From the *De Caelo* we learn that *pneuma* is indestructible (269A–298B). Evidently Aristotle holds that what distinguishes human beings from other animals is the mind accompanying the *pneuma*, whose vehicle is the semen of the male. Moreover, the "indestructible" *pneuma* parallels the "immortal and everlasting" active mind, and both are agents. Most likely, the kind of immortality that Aristotle the biologist ascribes to the active mind parallels that of *pneuma*. This is possessed by all living things, the vegetable, animal, and human being: "It is the most natural function in living things . . . to produce another thing like themselves in order that they may partake of the everlasting and divine . . . and what persists is not the thing itself but something like itself, not the specimen but the species" (15AB).

This conception of immortality is much the same as that described by Diotima in Plato's *Symposium*: "This is how every mortal creature perpetuates itself. It cannot, like the divine, be still the same throughout eternity: it can only leave behind new life to fill the vacancy that is left in its species by obsolescence" (208A).

The preceding conceptions shed light on the penultimate phrases: "but we do not remember because this is not acted upon, whereas the passive mind is perishable. . . ." Since the active mind does not remember or think, and since the passive mind is dependent upon the former for these activities and is perishable, there is no memory of "our" previous existence.

These conceptions also lead to a satisfactory interpretation of the puzzling last five words of the passage: "and without this, thinks nothing" (*kai aneu toutou outhen noei*). The "this" could refer to either the passive or the active mind, while *outhen noei* could be read either as "thinks nothing" or as "nothing thinks."[17] We know that in procreation both the female and the male are necessary for conception, so "this" can mean either passive mind or active mind. But from Aristotle's overall attitude to procreation we can be almost sure that the parallel in the model is: "and without the male, the female cannot conceive." Since only the passive mind thinks, and since the active mind is needed to actualize potential thought, the passage reads ". . . and without the active mind, the passive mind does not think."

Aristotle's Androgynous Mind

That "the passive mind is perishable" is what one expects of a capacity of the body such as the central faculty of sense. Yet this appears to conflict with Aristotle's claim in the preceding chapter that if the mind were mixed with the body "it would have some organ like the faculty of sense; but in fact it has none" (29A 26–27). Since there is so little treatment of the faculty of sense in the *De Anima*, Aristotle probably intends that the mind does not have a special organ like one of the special organs of sense. Compare his remark: "It is impossible that there should be a special sense organ for the common objects" (25A 14–15). He might have continued: "It is possible, however, that there should be a common organ for the common objects." This possibility is realized in that central organ, the heart.

THE TRINITY

Aristotle's passive and active minds are both substances in two of his senses of the word. The former is a substratum, and the latter is a substance in the sense of essence. But in accounting for these two substances we must not ignore the presence of a third Aristotelian substance, the offspring of their intercourse. The active mind, for example, acts upon the passive mind to produce thought. Aristotle describes this process: "It lies in our power to think whenever we will" (*bouletai*) (17B).

The functional aspect of this trinity illuminates Aristotle's conception of the mind that "becomes all things" and the mind that "makes all things" and is "in essence activity." I take "all things" to mean any object that the pasive mind thinks. Just as the menses, when activated by the male, become the offspring, so the mind, which is only a capacity to think, or potentially its thoughts, becomes its thoughts when activated by the active mind. "That part of the soul which we call 'mind' (by 'mind' I mean that part by which the soul thinks and forms judgments) has no actual existence until it thinks" (29A 23–4). There is, then, no conflict between Aristotle's remark in the preceding chapter, "Mind

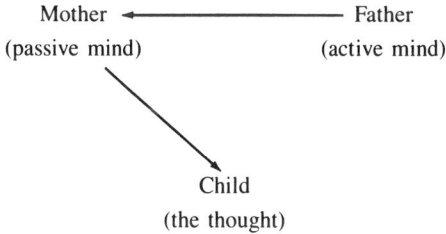

Fig. 3.5. Aristotle's trinity

does not always think" (30A6–7), and the paradox in the present, "Mind always thinks" (30A 22–23). In the former, passive mind is a mere capacity waiting to be activated by the active mind. In the latter, what was a mere capacity has now been actualized; mind has become its thoughts. This is the move from potency and power to actuality, and the stress is on the last member of the trinity. This is what we expect of Aristotle the biologist, who holds that "the business of most animals is nothing else than to produce young" (*GA* 717A).

CONCLUSION: THE END OF THE SEARCH FOR ORIGINS

It seems likely to me that the traditional subject-predicate and substance-attribute theories of mind rise from the contributions of Aristotle. It seems to me just as likely that these are nothing but modifications of the Procreation Model that Aristotle developed from the work of his teacher Plato. Certainly Aristotle was the first to spell out in any detail the main features of the subject-predicate relation—features we still take for granted today. Some of these features I have noted in the first chapter. Others will be used and questioned in the next. As we shall see, Aristotle distinguishes between two of the central concepts he uses to divide up all that exist. These are *in a subject* and *predicated of a subject*. In each case he is talking about the same subject, for he uses the same word, *hypokeimenon*, and he claims that some of the things that are in a subject are also predicated of a subject. As we have seen, the feature *in a subject* is at the center of the process of procreation. So central is it that Plato and Aristotle based much of their accounts of the Receptacle and the mind, respectively, upon it. They wanted a relation such that things can be in a subject without being a part of it. Subjects of predicates, on the other hand, tend to merge into parts and thus to "collapse into" their predicates. At the start of his book Aristotle says that "the body cannot be soul, since the body is not something predicated of a subject but is to be regarded as a subject, that is, as matter" (12B). This suggests that the soul is to be predicated. Such a view of Aristotle, as we shall see, leads to consequences regarding future subject-predicate theories.

How does Aristotle's theory relate to these traditional subject-predicate theories? In the first chapter of this book we found that the mind or soul or person has been treated in our tradition as a subject or substance in the sense of a substratum (*hypokeimenon*). Such a view seems to be modeled not upon Aristotle's active mind but upon his passive mind, or *nous pathetikos*.

Aristotle's Androgynous Mind

But in this chapter we have found that the soul, although it is a substance (*ousia*), is not a subject or substratum at all. The soul is a substance in the sense of being the form (*eidos*) of a natural body. This soul or form is the active power or life-force distinguishing living creatures from non-living ones.

We can now see more clearly what the nature of this soul is. In the plant, the primary soul, or the form of the plant, is not just nutrition or reproduction. It is the active power to nourish and to reproduce. Our word "soul," the usual translation of "*psyche*," fails to capture such an active power. One that more nearly captures it is "life-force." Similarly, the primary soul of animals is not just perception but the active power or mind-force to perceive, while in humans the primary soul is not the passive capacity to think but the active power that can create a thought, and it is called *nous poietikos*. At the end of *De Anima* Aristotle uses a feature from the Craftsman Model to illustrate this active power: "The soul acts like the hand; for just as a hand is a tool of tools, so the mind is a form of forms" (31B). Clearly he is referring to an active and not a passive power, for elsewhere he compares tools to semen: "Nature uses the semen as a tool . . . just as tools are used in the products of any art . . ." (*GA* 30B). The associations with active and indestructible *pneuma* have already been noted (cf. Plato's *Divine Seed*).

When Socrates, about to die, replied to Crito's question about where to bury him, "Anywhere you like if you can catch me," it is likely that he thought of his soul not as a substratum but as an active substance like *pneuma*. When Jesus, about to die on the cross, uttered, "Father, into thy hands I commend my spirit," he was saying, according to the original version of St. Luke's Gospel: "Father, into thy hands I commend my *pneuma;*" and when he "gave up the ghost" he was giving up his *pneuma*. This *pneuma* is substance (*ousia*), but it is not a subject or substratum. It is substance in the sense of essence. Since it is also spirit or *pneuma* it is called by some "spiritual substance." Defenders of the view that the mind or soul or self is spiritual substance are rare. Fortunately, there is at least one such defender, but we have to wait a long time after Aristotle to find him. Let us leap forward 2000 years to consider Berkeley, one of the few defenders of spiritual substance in our modern era, one who is probably alone in defending it at the same time as he rejects the subject-predicate theory.

During the next two millennia after Plato and Aristotle, the two great progenitors of so much of our conceptual scheme, the metaphor of procreation, having done its job, largely disappeared from mention in the writings of the great philosophers. But the effects of its early application remained alongside and partially embedded in the traditional substance-attribute theories of mind and matter.

Our search for the origins of the creative mind and the substance-attribute theory of mind has now ended. In Plato's Procreation Model, I believe, we find the sources of both of these. But it was Aristotle who first applied the model and made what was potential into the actual. He produced a theory of mind and devised a substance-attribute, subject-predicate distinction, both derived, if I am right, from the Procreation Model. We notice at once, however, that although the latter derives from the Procreation Model, it fails to provide some basic features present in Aristotle's own account of the mind, especially the feature of intercourse between two entities to produce a joint product, a "procreation feature," as we have noticed, that is basic in modern physics: Physical phenomena are the products of interaction of energy with matter. We have already noticed the lack of balance in substance-attribute theories as regards activity and passivity that does not appear in theories derived from the Procreation Model.

Aristotle barely uses the conception of substance-attribute in his *De Anima*. His theory is based on the parent of this model. He does indicate, however, that the human soul, that is, the active mind, is a substance in the sense of essence but not in the sense of substratum. If we look forward to Descartes' theory, we find that the soul or mind is also a substance, but it is a substance in the sense of substratum, a subject of predicates and of inherence. As we have seen, Aristotle holds that the soul is, rather, the form that inheres in that subject. Accordingly, Aristotle is not responsible for the alteration and mistake made by posterity, perhaps owing to the word magic present in the ambiguity of the word "substance" and its correlatives in other European languages deriving from Latin. The mistake probably would not have occurred if the Procreation Model had been before the minds of subsequent philosophers. This, in turn, would have been more likely if Aristotle's *Generation of Animals* had been required reading for students of the *De Anima*.

CHAPTER 4

Resuscitating the Metaphor I:
Berkeley's Understanding and Will

All talk concerning the soul is altogether or for the most part, metaphorical.

George Berkeley

Although the Procreation Model has long since gone underground, its influence as an archetype persists. The effects of this influence are visible in the writings of modern philosophers but most clearly seen in Berkeley and Kant. Plato and Aristotle had at their disposal the powerful tools of the Procreation Model, but Berkeley probably did not. We shall see, however, that he was familiar with the *Timaeus* and the *De Anima*. In this chapter, I identify three main tenets of Berkeley's philosophy: the Distinction Principle, which says that the mind is entirely distinct from its ideas; the Inherence Principle, which says that ideas exist only in the mind; and the Identity Principle, which says that an idea is not distinct from the idea perceived; principles that posterity has judged to be irreconcilable, thus constituting a radical incoherence at the very heart of Berkeley's theory. Using the Procreation Model, I try to show that these principles are consistent, just as they are in the systems of Plato and Aristotle. Indeed it is *as if* these three principles, central in Berkeley's philosophy, are direct applications of the Procreation Model. Thus I can suggest that Berkeley's doctrine of spiritual substance is able to withstand the skeptical refutations of subsequent thinkers beginning with Hume. In my account I reveal Berkeley's novel way of keeping the mind as a subject of inherence while rejecting the notion that it is a subject of predication.

Modern philosophy is sometimes characterized as a gradual abandoning of the metaphysics of substance. It is usual to begin with Descartes, who set down two distinct substances and formulated the traditional mind/body dichotomy. With Hume, less than a century later, we reach a logical conclusion in the disappearance of the two substances and, a fortiori, the disappearance of a metaphysics of substance.

Berkeley occupies an interesting position in this "history of substance." Although at heart he has the same ulterior motive as Descartes, to keep mind as substance, he shares Hume's desire to drop matter as substance. And since Anglo-American philosophy sees Hume as one of its great forebears while regarding Descartes as the father of modern philosophy, Berkeley is commonly regarded either as a halfhearted Humean or worse, a "castrated Cartesian."[1]

Berkeley's middle stance, with its apparent inconsistencies, is all the more untenable because of the noticeably brief treatment he gives mind substance and the relation of mind to ideas. As a result of the cursory mention of mind in Berkeley's extant works (an incomplete treatise on the mind was lost during his travels), it remains for sympathetic commentators to fill the gaps, to reconcile seeming contradictions, and to re-create a picture more complete than Berkeley's.

My belief is that Berkeley's half-hidden doctrine of mind substance belongs to the ancient tradition described earlier in this book, a connection that has been overlooked. It is my belief also that if Berkeley's doctrine is restored to this tradition, many of the issues surrounding his account of mind substance may be illuminated and the problems solved. Not a Cartesian tradition—the roots are different—it begins with Plato and Aristotle, who formulated the notion of a substance entirely distinct from its qualities yet itself capable of supporting those qualities.

PROBLEMS

Some of the main difficulties in the interpretation of Berkeley's account of mind and its relation to ideas appear in his very first statements on these topics early in the *Principles*.[2] In section 2 he asserts:

> This perceiving, active being is what I call "mind," "spirit," "soul," or "myself." By which words I do not denote any one of my ideas, but a thing *entirely distinct from* them, *wherein they exist* or, which is the same thing, whereby they are perceived—for the existence of an idea consists in being perceived.

These are statements, not arguments.[3] They suggest that Berkeley is introducing axioms or principles that refer to primitive entities, thus explaining other matters while remaining themselves unexplained. The mind is one of these primitive entities, "a thing," a substance, but not so-called until several sections later. Mind is a "perceiving active being," suggesting a substance both passive and active, although this is not clearly indicated until much later in the book. Berkeley then introduces two important principles, one of which I call the Distinction Principle:[4] The mind is entirely distinct from ideas; and the other the Inherence Principle: Ideas exist only in the mind. Although Berkeley begins to clarify the meaning of the latter, he leaves the relationship between the two principles begging for clarification for the two are apparently inconsistent. How can ideas be entirely distinct from the mind and yet not exist unless they are in it? In section 5, Berkeley introduces a third principle and in doing so appears to contradict himself once more. He asserts that it is impossible to conceive "any sensible thing or object distinct from the sensation or perception of it." In the same section he asks and answers the question: "Is it possible to separate, even in thought, any of these [ideas or impressions] from perception? For my part, I might as easily divide a thing from itself." I call this the Identity Principle: The perceiving of an idea is not distinct from the idea perceived. The Identity Principle appears to contradict the Distinction Principle because we seem to have been told that perceiving is part of the mind itself. How can ideas be entirely distinct from the mind although not distinct from being perceived by the mind?

SOLUTIONS

These passages have been much discussed and diversely interpreted in recent years. Of the Distinction Principle A. A. Luce says, "This distinction is in the ground-plan of the book, in its very fabric."[5] But Luce's stance is shared by few. In the traditional view, as we shall see, the Distinction Principle must be dropped in order to make Berkeley's system consistent.

The Inherence Principle has always been near the forefront of discussion about Berkeley. Lately, however, it has received more critical attention from several scholars. Edwin B. Allaire, who revived the discussion, claims that Berkeley's idealism rests upon the Inherence Principle and that "Berkeley's rather simple mistake . . . is that he persists in claiming that qualities must inhere in a substance, even though he insists that they are not predicated of a substance."[6] Allaire presumably holds that if Berkeley corrected his mistake, he would claim that qualities inhere in mind substance *and* are predicated of that substance. But if predicated of mind substance, such qualities become parts of mind. Mind substance then would collapse into its qualities in the same way as material substance, as Berkeley himself shows. Thus we are forced to drop Berkeley's Distinction Principle and hold instead that the mind is a collection of qualities or ideas; that is, to adopt a Humean view of the mind.

The Identity Principle has been attacked throughout the twentieth century, beginning with G. E. Moore's celebrated attack on idealism.[7]

Moore claims that Berkeley's idealism rests ultimately upon this principle, and he argues that Berkeley contradicts himself within the principle. More recently, S. A. Grave and George Pitcher have drawn attention to the apparent inconsistency between the Distinction Principle and the Identity Principle although of course they regard the apparent inconsistency as a real one. Grave says: "Nothing would be more valuable in Berkeleian commentary than a reconciliation of these principles," and admits: "I regret having no suggestions to offer. The positions seem to be quite irreconcilable." Grave asks which of the two principles Berkeley "really held," and answers: "Berkeley did not hold two sets of conflicting opinions . . . ; he held the opinions prescribed by the Identity Principle." If this is so, then Berkeley must drop the Distinction Principle, "and the mind is thought of not as a substance but as a system"; and on this view, "ideas will have to become 'part of the mind'."[8] Pitcher notes the same "serious inconsistency," and argues that "the simplest and best way to preserve the largest bulk of Berkeley's central philosophical doctrines is to have him abandon [the Distinction Principle]." Pitcher has Berkeley adopt instead the view that ideas are "only weakly distinct from the mind" and adopt also the adverbial analysis instead of the act-object analysis required by the Distinction Principle.[9]

Thus in the traditional view neither the Inherence Principle nor the Identity Principle is consistent with the Distinction Principle (the last being close to common sense). Berkeley's system supposedly can be made consistent only if he drops the Distinction Principle and adopts an account of the mind paralleling his phenomenalist account of matter; that is, adopts a Humean view of the mind. A. J. Ayer, looking at Berkeley through Humean spectacles, states the logical decline succinctly: "The considerations which make it necessary, as Berkeley saw, to give a phenomenalist account of material things, make it necessary, as Berkeley did not see, to give a phenomenalist account of the self."[10]

It is not, I think, generally realized that Berkeley was fully aware of this apparent inconsistency and of the theory of mind that according to posterity, his own principles forced him to hold. Berkeley in fact anticipated this objection in 1734. Hylas, the materialist, says: "You must either admit matter or reject spirit." Since Philonous, the "mind lover," refuses to admit matter, Hylas administers the apparent coup de grace: "In consequence of your own principles it should follow that you are only *a system of floating ideas* . . . " (*Dialogues* III 4). Using principles as well as words like Berkeley's, Hume reached the same conclusion in 1739: "The mind," he claimed, "is *a system of different perceptions* [my italics]."[11] Unlike Berkeley, however, Hume accepted this conclusion, and thus, it is believed, made Berkeley consistent.

Firmly entrenched though it be, the traditional view is an unsatisfactory interpretation of Berkeley's philosophy. Subscribers must discard the fundamental facts that are Berkeley's singular tenets, thus giving us an emasculated Berkeley. In the following pages, as an alternative to the traditional view, I try to show that Berkeley's system is indeed consistent; that, in accord with what he intended, we can retain the Distinction Principle and refrain from adopting the Humean theory of mind.

"ACT" AND OBJECT

I shall consider first Berkeley's apparent contradiction between the Distinction and Identity principles. I begin with the Identity Principle, in which he asserts that perceiving an idea and the idea perceived are the same thing. The discussion of this topic develops from Berkeley's point of view the account given in chapter 3.

Most of us try to make a distinction between what philosophers call "the act" and "the object." Certainly we can find words to suit such a distinction: for example, between having a toothache and the toothache itself, or between hearing a sound and the sound we hear. Early in this century, however, G. E. Moore, in his famous article "The Refutation of Idealism" (1903), found it necessary to defend this distinction against its contrary notion: "To identify 'blue' or any other of what I have called 'objects' of sensation with the corresponding sensation is, in every case, a self-contradictory error."[12] Bertrand Russell, in his equally famous work, the *Problems of Philosophy* (1912), tried also to defend it: "This question of the distinction between *act* and *object* in our apprehending of things is vitally important, since our whole power of acquiring knowledge is bound up with it [my italics]."[13]

Berkeley, as we have seen, holds a position contrary to that of Moore and Russell. He expressed it succinctly in section 5 of the first edition of the *Principles*: "In truth the object and the sensation are the same thing and cannot, therefore, be abstracted from each other." This is perhaps the more important half of Berkeley's *esse-percipi* principle.

Let us see where this principle fits within Berkeley's conception of the structure and functions of the mind. The mind (or spirit) he tells us, is "one, simple, undivided, active being." Nevertheless, it is "passive as well as active," as defined by its "two principal powers." "As it perceives ideas it is called 'the Understanding,' and as it produces or otherwise operates about them it is called 'the Will' " (*Principles* 27,

Correspondence IV 3). What are powers? Here Berkeley subscribes to an ancient tradition begun by Plato of distinguishing passive and active powers (faculties or capacities). Since a faculty (*dynamis*) cannot be perceived, it is identified by its activities and objects (*Republic* 477D). Sensation, for example, is a passive capacity. Whenever there is intercourse between any sense organ with a passive capacity and an appropriate external object possessing an active power "there arise offspring, endless in number but in pairs of twins. One twin is the perceiving [for example, the activity of seeing or hearing], whose birth always coincides with that of the other twin, the thing perceived [that is, the object, for example, a color or a sound]" (*Theaetetus* 156). Aristotle goes further: "When that which can hear is actually hearing, and when that which can sound is sounding, then the actual hearing and the actual sound are merged in one"; and "The activity (*energeia*) of the [external] object and that of the sense faculty is the same" (*De Anima* 425B, 426A).

These features of passive and active powers and their twin activities reappear in Berkeley's concept of mind. Thus the Understanding (that is, the thing standing under), is the passive capacity of supporting ideas or of being a substance or subject in the sense of substratum, whereas the Will is an active power of creating ideas or of being a substance in the sense of essence or *ousia*. In so-called acts of imagination, my will acts upon my understanding to produce ideas of imagination, which are creations or "creatures of my will." In sensation, a will external to mine (cf. Plato's and Aristotle's external object) acts upon my understanding to produce ideas of sense (colors, sounds, smells, tastes, and feels), which are "not creatures of my will" but creations of "some other will." In perception, the two wills—God's and mine—produce "collections of ideas constitut[ing] a stone, a tree, a book, and the like sensible things," my will doing the collecting and combining since "number is entirely the creature of the mind" (*Principles* 1, 12, 28, 29). The second of these unions of Understanding and Will, specifically sensation, concerns the Principle of Identity. Berkeley considers here only the second of Plato's twins, the object or the idea perceived (for example, a color or a sound), the merger of the object with the activity having been argued for at *Principles* 5.

How do we decide between the position held by Moore and Russell and its contrary held by Berkeley, Plato, and Aristotle? We do so, I think, partly by introspection. Berkeley asks us, in effect, to carry out the *Gedankenexperimente* of trying to abstract, for example, my having a toothache from the toothache I have, or my seeing a color from the color

I see (*Principles* 5). He thinks that it cannot be done and that in thinking we can achieve this feat we are the victims of words. Moreover, whereas Moore and Russell hold that in the act of sensing we are active, Berkeley, Plato, and Aristotle hold that we are entirely passive. Berkeley thinks this issue also is resolved by introspection. At *Dialogues* I, 9, Berkeley makes Philonous argue convincingly that while sniffing a rose I am active, but in smelling it I am passive. He says that the sniffing cannot be called "smelling," "for if it were I should smell every time I breathed in that manner." Lending a hand to Philonous, one can see that Moore and Russell are victims of word magic. Aristotle's *energeia* is often translated in the present context as "activity," erroneously suggesting to readers the notions of act and agency. Thus the mind has been regarded mistakenly as active or as an agent in having sensations. Aristotle's *energeia* also is translated often as "actuality," or the opposite of potentiality. This is the way Berkeley takes it in *Principles* 5, where he uses such phrases as "actually perceived" and "actual sensation."

Moore and Russell subsequently reversed their views and adopted this part of Berkeley's *esse-percipi* principle. Russell was the first to change, writing in 1921: "The possibility of distinguishing the sensation from the sense datum vanishes. . . . Accordingly, the sensation that we have when we see a patch of colour simply is that patch of colour, an actual constituent of the physical world, and a part of what physics is concerned with."[14] Moore's change of view in 1941 is certain but not so definite: "A toothache certainly cannot exist without being felt, but . . . on the other hand, the moon certainly can exist without being perceived."[15] In his original refutation Moore intended to show that Berkeley's mistake lay in the identification of sensations with their objects, as in the toothache example and Russell's color example. Accordingly, his retraction, following Russell's, indicates his withdrawal of the charge that Berkeley's Identity Principle contained a self-contradictory error.

We are more concerned, however, with another supposed contradiction. We examined the Identity Principle to find out whether it could possibly conflict with the Distinction Principle. As the preceding account makes obvious, the two principles are perfectly compatible: In his Distinction Principle, Berkeley states that the mind is entirely distinct from ideas. We now see that in terms of faculties or capacities and their actualities, or powers and their effects, Berkeley is claiming that the mind with its capacities belongs to an entirely different category from its actualities or effects.

This interpretation opposes Grave and Pitcher, who maintain that Berkeley contradicts himself in holding both of these principles. Although the issue is now defined, it is helpful to summarize the main points.

First, *Principles* 2 and 27 clarify that the mind or spirit is not the same as its two principal powers or faculties or capacities, namely, the Understanding and the Will. Rather the mind has or possesses these powers. This view of Berkeley differs from Gilbert Ryle's, who in his *Concept of Mind*[16] holds that the mind is (that is, is nothing but) its powers, "abilities," or "dispositions," and that it is the person, or perhaps the body, that has or possesses them.

Second, according to the Distinction Principle, the mind with its powers or faculties is specifically distinct or heterogeneous from its actualities or activities (that is, from its ideas "actually perceived" or its "actual sensations[s]" [*Principles* 5]). In the phrase "This perceiving, active being" of *Principles* 2, the words "perceiving" and "active " refer to powers or faculties; whereas the words "being perceived," "actually perceived," etc., of *Principles* 5 refer to activities or actualities. The two sorts or kinds are "more distant and heterogeneous from [each other] than light is from darkness" (*Principles* 141); they are what we might call nowadays different logical types or categories.

Third, according to the Identity Principle, the so-called act and the object—the supposedly different actualities or activities—are identical when the mind is actually undergoing or receiving them. They are passive "activities."

Fourth, in the light of the second and third points, obviously Berkeley can hold consistently both the Distinction and the Identity principles. In the former he is distinguishing heterogeneous items (items from two different categories); whereas in the latter he is identifying items within one category. To some extent, Berkeley invites the charge of inconsistency for he does not clearly indicate in *Principles* 2 that the words "being perceived," "perception," etc., refer to the exercise or actuality of that power or faculty. But when we consider all his utterances, especially those of *Principles* 27, his meaning becomes clear.

PLATO'S RECEPTACLE AND BERKELEY'S MIND

To test the inconsistency supposed to exist in Berkeley's system between the Distinction and Inherence principles I shall use two well-known methods. The first is to reduce the theory to another more firmly established theory—one whose consistency, though not necessarily con-

Berkeley's Understanding and Will 75

tent, is generally accepted. The second is to find a familiar interpretation of the structure of the theory in which the commonplace statements are true—in effect, to find a model. Because a model is simply an alternative interpretation of the calculus of a theory, both methods use models.[17]

I present Berkeley's system in terms of a wholly different subject presented by Plato in the second part of the *Timaeus*: the Receptacle "and, as it were, the Nurse of all Becoming and change" (49A), which Plato later calls "space."[18] Since the things that enter the Receptacle (images of the Forms) are "fleeting, changeable entities, they cannot be designated as 'this thing' or 'that thing' but only as 'of a certain quality'" (49D, E). Only the Receptacle itself "wherein all of these qualities come to exist . . . deserves the names 'this thing' and 'that thing' " (49E, 50). The Receptacle, with its stability and receptivity, models Berkeley's mind substance, while the fleeting and changeable qualities within the Receptacle model Berkeley's ideas. This distinction enables me to clarify the puzzling relationship between Berkeley's two principles:

Plato	Berkeley
The things entering [the Receptacle] . . . are of an entirely distinct kind (*parapan alles physeos*) (*Timaeus* 50E).	[A mind] is a thing entirely distinct from [its ideas] wherein they exist (*Principles* 2).
It is proper that an image . . . should come into existence in something else, clinging to existence as best it may, on pain of being nothing at all (*Timaeus* 52C).	[Ideas] are . . . fleeting, dependent beings which subsist not by themselves, but are supported by or exist in minds or spiritual substances (*Principles* 89).

In *Principles* 89 Berkeley's statement of the Distinction Principle is even more emphatic. He distinguishes "two kinds entirely distinct and heterogeneous, . . . to wit, spirits and ideas." Just as there is no contradiction in holding that physical qualities must exist in space although they are not a part of space, so there is none in holding that ideas can exist only in a mind although they are not a part of mind.

Since I have assumed that Plato's account is consistent, it is advisable to go farther back to a more concrete and familiar model against which we can test both Plato's and Berkeley's theories. Fortunately, Plato himself provides the model. He likens the Receptacle and the Becoming (that is, any of the phenomena) to a mother and her child, respectively and probably also to their essential biological features, the womb and the embryo (*Timaeus* 50D, 91D). Just as the embryo is entirely distinct from but cannot exist without the womb in which it exists, so ideas are entirely distinct from but cannot exist without the mind in which they exist.

This solution is independent of whether Berkeley was aware of the parallel between Plato's Receptacle and his own concept of mind. Other parallels, however, confirm the view of Berkeley's first biographer, Joseph Stock: "His favourite author from whom many of his notions were borrowed was Plato."[19] They confirm the view also that Berkeley was familiar with the *Timaeus*.

ARISTOTLE'S SUBJECT AND BERKELEY'S MIND

The apparent inconsistency of *Principles* 2 recurs in the famous Fifth Objection of *Principles* 49. On the latter occasion, however, Berkeley assumes the first of his suspect principles, "Mind is entirely distinct from ideas," and tries to anticipate an objection to his second suspect principle, "Ideas exist only in the mind": "It may perhaps be objected that if extension and figure exist only in the mind, it follows that the mind is extended and figured, since extension is a mode or attribute which (to speak with the Schools) is predicated of the subject in which it exists." Here Berkeley deduces an apparent but, to him, mistaken consequence from his Inherence Principle: The ideas largeness and squareness, for example, exist only in the mind; therefore the mind is large and square. It has been customary to accept Berkeley's objection against himself as his real view because the consequences he deduces from his Inherence Principle look irresistible. Bertrand Russell, for example, sustains Berkeley's objection and comments: "This confusion may seem too gross to have been really committed by any competent philosopher."[20]

Berkeley begins his defense: "I answer, those qualities are in the mind only as they are perceived by it—that is, not by way of *mode* or *attribute*, but only by way of *idea*." This answer appears inadequate where it stands but not so when moved to the conclusion of the following argument, in which Berkeley sets up rival interpretations of the simple proposition: "A die is hard, extended, and square." The interpretation of the "philosophers" is: "They will have it that the word 'die' denotes a *subject* or *substance* distinct from the hardness, extension, and figure which are *predicated of* it, and *in which* they exist."

Berkeley's Understanding and Will

Berkeley here sketches a traditional doctrine of Western philosophy, according to which the subject-predicate distinction in logic and grammar parallels the substance-attribute dichotomy in ontology. Thus the subject "die" and the substance *die* are "distinct from" their predicates and attributes, respectively; they are "complete," "self-subsistent" entities that can "stand alone"; whereas the corresponding predicates and attributes are "incomplete," "dependent" entities.[21] Berkeley calls this interpretation "groundless and unintelligible." It is easy to see why he rejects it. First, if it is true, then materialism is true, for the die is a material substance, "an inert, senseless substance in which extension, figure, and motion do actually subsist" (*Principles* 9). Second, to use the substance *die* as a model for the substance *mind* would be disastrous. Certainly Berkeley holds of the word "mind," just as philosophers hold "die," that it "denotes a subject or substance distinct from the hardness, extension, and figure . . . and in which they exist." But he cannot hold that these qualities are predicated of the subject "mind" without being forced, as many think he is, to adopt a Humean view of mind or to commit the gross confusion noted by Russell. Therefore, Berkeley gives a different interpretation of the proposition: "To me a die seems to be nothing distinct from those things which are termed its modes or accidents. And to say a die is hard, extended, and square is not to attribute those qualities to a subject distinct from and supporting them, but only an explication of the meaning of the word 'die'."

In this short passage Berkeley sketches a new theory of predication or, since he drops the subject-predicate distinction, a rival theory, which I have called the *definiendum-definiens* theory.[22] He dispenses with the "is" of predication and replaces it with the "is" of identity, thus interpreting the proposition not as a subject-predicate proposition but a *definiendum-definientes* expression. He is aware that a *definiendum* names no new entity distinct from those entities named by the *definientes*. By discarding the subject-predicate logic Berkeley also drops the parallel substance-attribute ontology. He adopts a "no-substance" theory by claiming that a die is the same as "its qualities" and can be analyzed into "its qualities."

On the face of it, as an argument for a new theory of mind, *Principles* 49 achieves the opposite of what Berkeley intends. By showing how the subject "die" collapses into its predicates or the substance *die* into its attributes, Berkeley appears to reinforce the objection against himself. If this argument demolishes material substance, then it should demolish mind substance as well, and Berkeley should end once again with a phenomenalist theory of mind. He appears to give the game away to Hume. Berkeley must show that sensible qualities, although mind-dependent, are not attributes of mind. Thus his overall problem is the same as before: If fleeting sensible qualities must cling to existence in the mind on pain of being nothing at all, how can they remain entirely distinct from it? This amounts to perhaps the major problem of Berkeley's philosophy in his defense against Humean skepticism: How, in answer to Hylas of *Dialogues* III 4, can he consistently reject matter and admit spirit? Although Berkeley concludes the debate on this subject between Hylas and Philonous with the words, "there is, therefore, upon the whole, no parity of case between spirit and matter," hardly anyone has accepted this conclusion.[23]

In order to see whether Berkeley can hold consistently that mind substance does not collapse into the sensible qualities which exist in it while material substance does collapse into its qualities, let us consider Berkeley's startling paradox in the light of Aristotle's account of predication and inherence in *Categories* II. Here is an occurrence of the remarkable juxtaposition of Distinction and Inherence principles such as we found in Berkeley's *Principles* 2. This peculiar marriage of two such apparently incompatible relations as entire distinction and "complete" inherence, which occurs in Plato's cosmology and cosmogony and, much later, in Berkeley's psychology and ontology, is not unexpected in Aristotle's logic and ontology.

At the start of his fourfold classification of "the things there are," Aristotle defines "in a subject": "By 'in a subject' (*en hypokeimeno*) I mean what is in something not as a part but which cannot exist apart from what it is in."[24] As we have seen with the help of Plato's account of things in the Receptacle, Berkeley needs precisely this conjunction of relations to model the peculiar relations of sensible ideas to minds. But if Aristotle's "in a subject" captures all that Berkeley needs (that is, if the inherence relation includes the distinction relation), is not Berkeley's assertion of the Distinction Principle redundant? The answer, I believe, is that Berkeley wants to stress the distinction relation. As we have seen, the ideas in the mind belong to a different category from the mind, and as Aristotle holds, the things in a subject belong to a category other than substance.

Aristotle now appears to complicate the matter unnecessarily, however, by conjoining the inherence relation with a new relation: predication. He classifies all existing things into those which are

Berkeley's Understanding and Will 79

a) predicated of a subject but are in no subject;
b) predicated of no subject but are in a subject;
c) predicated of a subject and also are in a subject;
d) neither predicated of a subject nor in a subject.

The class of existing things into which the "philosophers" put the qualities of material substances, as reported by Berkeley, is readily apparent. This class is defined by Aristotle's (c), for the philosophers hold that the qualities of the subject "die" are predicated of it and exist in it. Descartes subscribes to this view: "When we say that any attribute is contained in the nature or concept of anything, that is precisely the same as saying that it is true of that thing or can be affirmed of it."[25] But the philosophers only appear to subscribe to (c), for they deviate from Aristotle in holding that if something exists in a subject, then it is predicated of that subject. Aristotle's example, "Knowledge is in a subject, the soul, and is also predicated of a subject, knowledge-of-grammar," indicates that two different subjects are involved. Moreover, Aristotle holds, as in (b), that some things are in a subject although they are not predicated of any subject.

The class of existing things into which Berkeley puts sensible qualities is equally apparent. This class is defined by Aristotle's (b), for Berkeley holds that sensible qualities "are predicated of no subject but are in some subject [the mind]." Each of them is in such a subject "not as a part, but [as that] which cannot exist apart from what it is in"; or, as Berkeley concludes, they are in a subject, the mind, "not by way of *mode* or *attribute* but only by way of idea." Aristotle's examples of the members of class (b) are "some particular grammatical knowledge" and "a particular white." Because these are particular or individual they cannot be predicated, and they cling to existence only in something else. These atomic particulars of Aristotle's second example constitute Berkeley's simple ideas or sensible qualities. Both Aristotle and Berkeley leave unclear whether or not such atomic simples are nonrecurrent particulars or are particular in being determinate in kind (for example, in being determinate shades of color, etc., that are recurrent and can exist in more than one mind). It is likely, however, that Berkeley intends that his "certain color, taste, smell figure, and consistence" of *Principles* 1 can occur in several minds and not just in "this or that particular mind" (*Principles* 48).

Whether these qualities are recurrent or nonrecurrent is beside our main question regarding the consistency of the Distinction and Identity principles. This question has been largely answered. Berkeley's two principles can be regarded as a direct application of Aristotle's Inherence theory, whose consistency, though not entire contents, is generally accepted. Furthermore, Berkeley's attempted demolition of material substance (by showing that the substance *die* collapses into its predicates) does not demolish mind substance as well, because things that exist in the subject [mind] are not predicated of any subject. It is now generally accepted that such subjects, being individuals, can never be predicated. Moreover, Berkeley's two principles of *Principles* 2, as well as the two corresponding relations in Aristotle's and Plato's theories can be further tested for consistency by using Plato's Procreation Model of the *Timaeus*. Although Berkeley used some of Aristotle's notions effectively, he differed from him in a fundamental respect. Berkeley was ahead of his time in attempting to explode the Subject-Predicate Myth.

Most significantly, however, since Berkeley can hold without contradiction his three important principles of Distinction, Inherence, and Identity, he can refrain from adopting the Humean theory of mind, which, according to posterity, he is forced to accept.

CONCLUSION: BERKELEY'S ANDROGYNOUS MIND

We can see how Berkeley modifies the systems of Plato and Aristotle to make his own theory. He appears to adopt Aristotle's distinction between passive and active minds, calling them the Understanding and the Will, respectively. But while Aristotle's passive mind becomes its objects, Berkeley's Understanding remains entirely distinct from the ideas in it, thus enabling Berkeley to escape the Humean charge that the subject "mind" collapses into its predicates. Probably Aristotle's passive mind is modeled upon the placenta, whereas Berkeley's Understanding is modeled upon Plato's Receptacle (the womb). Moreover, Berkeley's active mind, which he calls the Will, is given the status of a faculty, which is a magnification of Aristotle's "willing." Berkeley uses some of Aristotle's words: "I find I can excite ideas in my mind at pleasure. . . . It is no more than willing. . . . This making and unmaking of ideas does very properly denominate the mind active" (*Principles* 22; cf. *De Anima* 27b). At this stage Berkeley proceeds to enlarge the human Understanding and Will to make his view of the nature of God, a being who combines the Good of Plato's *Republic* and the Father of the *Timaeus* with the Receptacle of the latter work, that is, an all-powerful creator combined with a mind that comprehends and contains all things, the space of the Receptacle being converted to a mind. This androgynous mind is similar to a large-scale version of the combination of Aristotle's passive and active minds with the difference noted above.[26]

We shall now see how Kant's theory of mind fits with the Platonic-Aristotelian faculty psychology and with the Procreation Model.

CHAPTER 5

Resuscitating the Metaphor, II:
Kant's Passive and Active Mind

The systems of the universe have been formed and produced out of the originally diffused primitive stuff that constitutes all the matter that filled empty space, the infinite receptacle of the divine presence.

Immanuel Kant

In this chapter I have three purposes. First, in order to emphasize that the effects of the Procreation Model continue into our modern era in spite of the fact that conscious use of it has long since disappeared, I offer one more illustration of its application to the structure and operations of the mind. This example (in spite of some limitations) is for my purposes one of the best available. Even though Kant uses its features unwittingly, the fecundity of the model is obvious in Kant's novel theory including his accounts of passive and active minds; potentiality and actuality; and objects of perception and knowledge seen as joint products of prior operations; as well as in his discussion of faculties. Equally obvious is that Kant's thinking is firmly ensconced in the Platonic-Aristotelian tradition. Although the metaphor in Kant's work has gone underground, I try to bring it into the light of day. Second, using the Procreation Model as well as parts of the Craftsman Model, I try to elicit the main features of the active mind, or what may be called "the Copernican Mind," following Kant's "Copernican Revolution" in philosophy. Such features include the powers of working up the raw material of sensation into knowledge, combining or separating, and making objects conform to our minds rather than the reverse. While Kant shared with Berkeley a mind-centered universe, though in different ways, it was in introducing the power of the creative mind that Berkeley paved the way for Kant and may have influenced him.[1] Third, I suggest that Kant weakens his theory when he presents it in terms of the traditional subject-predicate and substance-attribute conceptions.

THE PASSIVE SENSIBILITY AND THE ACTIVE UNDERSTANDING

In the opening of the *Critique of Pure Reason*, in order to formulate his well-known distinction between two sorts of knowledge, empirical and pure, Kant begins to draw a parallel distinction between two faculties, powers, or capacities of the mind, one of them a passive capacity, later called the "Sensibility," and the other an active power called the "Understanding":

> There can be no doubt that all our knowledge begins with experience. For how should our faculty of knowledge be awakened into action did not objects affecting our senses partly of themselves produce representations, partly rouse into activity the power of our understanding to compare these representations, and, by combining or separating them, work up the raw material of the sensible impressions into that knowledge of objects which is entitled experience? . . . But though all our knowledge begins with experience, it does not follow that it all arises out of experience. For it may well be that even our empirical knowledge is a compound of what we receive through impressions and of what our own faculty of knowledge (sensible impressions serving merely as the occasion) supplies from itself. (B1)[2]

Later we learn, on the one hand, that the Sensibility is "the receptivity of our mind, . . . the capacity for receiving representations through the mode of intuition in which we are affected by objects," and that by means of Sensibility "objects are given to us." We learn, on the other hand, that the Understanding is "the mind's power of knowing an object through these representations . . . of producing representations from itself, the spontaneity of knowledge"; that it enables us "to think the object of sensible intuition." Finally, we learn that these two powers are "two extremes," "distinct and separate," such that "the Understanding can intuit nothing, the senses can think nothing; only through their union can knowledge arise" (A19=B33, A51=B75, A124).

PROBLEMS

Several questions arise: What is the nature of these two faculties? Are they part of the furniture of the mind or merely theoretical devices? Compare Kant's "The Understanding is a faculty or power to act" with Gilbert Ryle's "The mind is a disposition to act."[3] Both philosophers use faculty or dispositional language, but whereas Ryle shows how to translate such statements into less mysterious language, Kant does not. What, then, is the appropriate interpretation of Kant? Does he provide a means for distinguishing one faculty from another? Does he distinguish passive capacities from active powers? Does his psychology of faculties help us understand the nature of the entity to which he refers in the phrase "this I or he or it (the thing) which thinks" (A346=B404)? Is this thing an agent or a patient or both? Does Kant's psychology of faculties help us understand the nature of his Copernican Revolution?

FACULTIES IN PLATO AND ARISTOTLE

We can answer these questions by once more using as paradigms the accounts given by Plato and Aristotle, who, like Kant, were faculty psychologists. Moreover, they have much the same "intellectual toolbox" containing such conceptual tools as matter and form, substance and accident, subject and inherence, active faculties and passive capacities, etc., tools created largely by Plato but given their neat labels by Aristotle.

Although Anaximander, Anaximenes, and Anaxagoras mentioned faculties or powers, Plato was the first I know of to give an account of and show how to detect and distinguish them. Faculties, he indicates, are either passive capacities to receive affections or active powers to produce effects. Recall that Plato says, "In a faculty I cannot find any of those qualities, such as color or shape, which [ordinarily] would enable me to distinguish one thing from another. I can only look to its *activities (apergazetai)* and to its field of objects, and regard these as enough to identify it" *(Republic* 477D). Sensation, for example, is a passive faculty that is identified by its activities and objects. Whenever there is union between our senses and the appropriate external object, that is, between a passive capacity and an active power, "there arise offspring endless in number but in pairs of twins" *(Theaetetus* 156). One twin is the activity of sensing, for example, seeing or hearing; the other is the sense datum, such as a color or a sound.[4]

As we have seen, Aristotle adopted this view of passive and active powers, including the method of identifying them by their twin activities. In the views of both Plato and Aristotle the so-called act in perceiving sense objects is a passive receiving.

What is the relevance of this to Kant? It is a priori likely that if Kant is speaking of faculties, then his account is similar in structure to the accounts of Plato and Aristotle. This is the case, although, as one expects, Kant uses a richer vocabulary and adds a few complications. If we look at the first pages of the *Aesthetic* we see that Kant's Sensibility, like Aristotle's sense faculty, is a passive capacity. Our Greek model

Kant's Passive and Active Mind 85

suggests that Kant's "intuition" is a passive activity, or better, that intuiting is a being acted upon, a passion, while agency belongs only to the external object that acts upon us. The Greek model suggests also that Kant's intuition is not an object but a process, properly represented in English not by the noun "intuition" but by the verbs "intuits" and "intuiting." However Kant at some times uses the noun, at others the verb. But if intuiting itself becomes an object of thought, the noun is dominant. Moreover, following the Greek model, Kant has three kinds of objects in his theory of perception: (1) the agent (as in his phrases "we are affected by objects" and "the effect of an object upon the faculty. . .") or an external object functioning as an efficient cause; (2) the object given prior to appearance (as in his phrase "Objects are given to us"); and (3) "the undetermined object of an empirical intuition," that is, the "appearance," presumably the synthesis of form and matter. One wonders at this stage: What makes the synthesis? The passive Sensibility? Aristotle holds that "the sense [faculty] receives the sensible *forms* of things without the matter" (24A), whereas Kant holds that "the form [of appearance] must lie ready for the sensations a priori in the mind."[5] This is not a significant difference, as we shall see.

KANT'S COPERNICAN REVOLUTION

Kant sets up his Copernican hypothesis as a rival to the traditional assumption: "Hitherto it has been assumed that all our knowledge must conform to objects . . . [Since this has failed] we must therefore make trial whether we may not have more success in the tasks of metaphysics if we suppose that objects must conform to our knowledge"(Bxvi). If we look at Kant's Copernican hypothesis from the standpoint of faculties or powers, that is, from the standpoint of ontology rather than epistemology, knowledge becomes a member of a causal series.

In that case, Kant's contribution is the claim that our knowledge of objects, far from being merely the effect upon our minds of external objects as causes, is a joint effect of these external causes and our minds. What I call the "Ptolemaic view" (our knowledge of objects is a passive reception of information from the external world as agent) and Kant's Copernican view are both causal theories of knowledge. However, in the Ptolemaic view knowledge is merely an effect, whereas in the Copernican view it is a product.

The roots of this Copernican Revolution can be seen in the Platonic-Aristotelian account of perception described in chapter 3. In this causal theory of perception, Sensibility is like a camera obscura with a screen at the back on which external objects make impressions. But this is to over-simplify. The roots of Kant's causal account of perception and, as we shall see, his causal theory of mind, can be traced back through his immediate precursors to Plato's cosmogony in the *Timaeus,* which had a rebirth at the end of the fifteenth century and provided Copernicus, Galileo, Kepler, and Newton with many ideas leading to the so-called the beginning of modern science. We have noted that in the *Timaeus* Plato elicits two sorts of powers, passive and active. The cosmos is their joint product. The divine Father creates (or the divine Craftsman constructs) this cosmos *from* a Pattern or Form *out of* Materials in the Receptacle of Space.[6] Kant was fully aware of this paradigm of Western thought, for he used it himself in his early work *The Theory of the Heavens,* published in 1755: "The systems of the universe," he says, "have been formed and produced out of the originally diffused primitive stuff that constitutes all the matter . . . that filled empty space, the infinite receptacle of the divine presence."[7] Here, lying ready in Kant's mind as well as in the *Timaeus,* a priori as it were, are the main tools he needs to start his Copernican Revolution. Note that the words "matter" and "receptacle" are derived from the concept of procreation. The analogue of this receptacle plays an important role in Aristotle's and Kant's theories of mind.

The Ptolemaic Mind

Newton also used Plato's Receptacle as a model for the minds or sensoriums, first of God, and then of human beings:

> Does it not appear from phenomena that there is a Being incorporeal, living, intelligent, omnipresent, who in infinite Space, as it were, in his Sensory, sees the things themselves intimately . . . by their immediate presence to himself: Of which things the Images only, carried through the Organs of Sense into our little sensoriums, are there seen and beheld by that which in us perceives and thinks.[8]

Using Newton's version of Plato's model I can sketch the "Ptolemaic theory of mind," a theory probably subscribed to by Galileo, Newton, and a host of others. Nature acts on our minds to produce images of external things in "our little sensoriums." The human mind is thus merely a passive capacity to receive into its receptacle copies of the archetypes in the remote external world. The only work the mind does is make guesses from these ectypes to the distant archetypes, things as they really are, without the distortions made in the mirrors of our little minds.

Kant's Passive and Active Mind

Corresponding to this Ptolemaic theory of mind is the doctrine Kant calls "Transcendental Realism," the view that objects "if they are to be external, must have an existence by themselves, and independently of the senses" (A369). If the passive subject were removed, these things in themselves would continue to exist in the Receptacle, that is, in absolute space and time though without any of the secondary qualities.

Kant's Initial Correction

Kant's initial correction of this theory is his account of the Sensibility; that is, his account of the human mind prior to the addition of the Understanding or, in terms of the sequence of his book, the Transcendental Aesthetic before the addition of the Transcendental Analytic: ". . . if the subject . . . be removed, the whole constitution and all the relations of objects in space and time, nay space and time themselves, would vanish. As appearances, they cannot exist in themselves, but only in us" (A42=B59).

Notice that the Sensibility is entirely a passive capacity to receive impressions from external objects, their efficient causes, things that exist in themselves but not in space and time. No activity in the sense of agency or cause occurs here, although that passive activity called intuition does occur as a function of Sensibility. What, then, of space and time, "its pure forms," which "inhere in our sensibility with absolute necessity" (A42–B60)? Kant says that these "lie ready for the sensations a priori in the mind" (A20=B34). They are, therefore, not causes or makers but inert potentialities lying ready to be activated and actualized by a cause or maker.

The Copernican Mind

It is easy now to elicit a main part of Kant's Copernican theory of mind. Kant appears to have first subtracted Plato's Craftsman and the Forms from external nature and then transferred them to the human mind as the active counterparts to our receptacles. Plato's Receptacle then reappears in the *Critique* as the Sensibility that is, as "the receptivity of our mind or its capacity to receive representations in so far as it is in any wise affected," while Plato's divine Craftsman and the Forms reappear as the Understanding, "the mind's power of producing representations from itself, the spontaneity of knowledge" and the categories, respectively (A51=B75).

Aristotle and Kant evidently subscribe to an imagist theory of thinking. Aristotle says that "the mind cannot think without an image," and

Kant holds that "we cannot think a line without drawing it in thought or a circle without describing it" (B154). If Kant conceives the Understanding as a skilled craftsman, one hopes he will reveal this image through concrete words. Fortunately, although the scenery of his mind, like that of Konigsberg, is sparse, this hope is realized in the well-known passage, already quoted, that opens his book. There we learn that Understanding, like a skilled craftsman, combines or synthesizes, separates, works up raw material into a product, is awakened into action, and contributes something else (skill or know-how?) that it "supplies from itself." Clearly the Understanding must be admitted into Kant's ontology as an efficient cause, that is, as an unmoved mover, a maker or producer like a craftsman. In the same passage Kant distinguishes causes of this type from "occasions" or occasional causes. Plato called such causes "second" or "auxiliary" causes, whereas Aristotle described them as "causes which move and are moved."

These two powers, the Sensibility and the Understanding, which Kant regards as entirely distinct, together with their product, knowledge of objects, constitute the main structure and furniture of the human mind. Clearly, although "these two powers or capacities cannot exchange their functions . . . , only through their union can knowledge arise" (A51–B75). The raw material that the Understanding works up into empirical knowledge is not, of course, the same raw material that was given to the external object in its role as agent or craftsman to work up into appearances. These appearances, products of the union of external cause with passive sensibility, constitute the raw material given by the Sensibility to the Understanding. Thus the Sensibility, after a brief encounter with the thing in itself, enters into a permanent marriage with the Understanding.

Kant tells us in the preface to his revolutionary book that in mathematics and physics similar revolutions resulted when great thinkers realized that the true method of science is not to inspect and describe the properties of external objects but "to bring out what was necessarily implied in the concepts that [they had themselves] formed a priori and had put into the figure . . . or into nature." Now in metaphysics Kant tells us that instead of supposing that "intuition [and thought] must conform to the constitution of objects," he will suppose that "the object [both as sensible and knowable] must conform to the constitution of our faculty of intuition [and faculty of understanding]" (Bxi–xvii). Usually Kant's achievement is put thus in epistemological terms or in the quasi-metaphysical terms, for example, of James Ward: "Kant exalted the

Kant's Passive and Active Mind

knowing subject and banished beyond the limits of knowledge the whole universe of things *per se*."⁹ Because Kant subscribes to what I call a causal theory of knowledge, I have presented his achievement as a metaphysical one: Kant subtracted the causal and organizing power from nature and transferred it to the human mind. He tells us at the end of *Transcendental Deduction* that he will now characterize the Understanding as "the faculty of rules." "Rules, so far as they are objective . . . are called laws. . . . Thus the Understanding is itself the Lawgiver of Nature" (A126). But since it has taken over much of the job of Plato's Craftsman we can characterize it as the Maker of Nature: "The order and regularity in the appearances, which we entitle *nature*, we ourselves introduce. We could never find them in appearances, had not we ourselves, or the nature of our mind, originally set them there (A125)."

"ARISTARCHUS" AND "COPERNICUS"

If Kant is the Copernicus of philosophy, then Aristotle is the Aristarchus. Just as Aristarchus in the third century B.C., according to Archimedes and Plutarch, supposed the sun-centered universe and thus anticipated the main discovery of Copernicus, so Aristotle anticipated the main premises of Kant's mind-centered metaphysics. Aristotle supposed that our knowledge of objects, far from being merely the effect of external causes upon our minds, is a joint product: first, of external causes and our minds and, second, of our active and passive minds.

To elicit similarities between Aristotle's views and Kant's I repeat some points from my account of Aristotle in chapter 3.

Aristotle's passive and active minds parallel Kant's passive Sensibility and active Understanding, respectively. Near the end of *De Anima* Aristotle formulates his famous distinction between passive mind *(nous pathetikos)* and active mind *(nous poietikos)* as the conclusion of an argument from analogy: "Since just as in the whole of nature there is something that serves as matter for each kind of thing (and this is what is potentially all of them), and something else which is their cause or agent because it makes them all—the two being related as a craft is to its material—so the same distinction must be found in the soul (30A)."

Compare this with Kant's distinction given on the first page of this chapter. Aristotle's passive mind is initially a capacity for receiving impressions made by external objects. Considering *Parva Naturalia* and *De Anima* together leads to the view that Aristotle's passive mind is none other than the primary sense faculty, or the Common Sense (50A). This faculty is similar to Kant's Sensibility.

Aristotle, like Kant, subscribes to a causal theory of perception: "[In perceiving we are acted upon]; the objects which can produce the actuality of perception are external to us"(17B). Kant describes this process thus: ". . . things as objects of our senses existing outside us are given. . . . they cause representations in us by affecting our senses . . . there are bodies without us [that have] influence on our sensibility. . . ." (*Prolegomena* Sec. 13)[10]

Aristotle and Kant make the well-known distinction between the act and the object, expressed in early twentieth-century philosophical vocabulary as the sensation and the sense datum or the perceiving and the percept. This is expressed by Aristotle as *aisthesis* and *aistheton* and by Kant as the *intuition* and the *given sensation*. Both differ from the views of such thinkers as Moore and Russell in holding that the act of perceiving is not an action but merely a passive receiving.

Aristotle and Kant differ from the views of these thinkers also in holding that during actual perception the perceiving and the percept are "merged in one" to become the "sensible object" or the "appearance."

How are such sensible objects related to the perceiving subject? The common answer, now so familiar, is that these objects exist *in* the subject. Recall that Aristotle says, "By *in a subject* I mean what is in something not as a part but which cannot exist apart from what it is in" (*Categories,* ch. II, cf. *Timaeus* 50–52). Kant says: "We cannot be sentient of what is outside ourselves but only of what is *in us*" (A 378); and "All appearances are not in themselves *things:* they are nothing but ideas, and cannot exist outside our mind" (A492 = B520).

Both men expound a duplication in the human mind of the feature of agency, power, or efficient cause already posited as a prominent feature of the external world. This completes the duplication in the mind of the two powers in the external world described in Plato's *Timaeus*. The human mind is thus a proposed microcosm of the postulated macrocosm. But whereas Plato used the vocabulary of "craftsman," "materials," "receptacle," and "product" for the macrocosm, Aristotle and Kant use only some of this vocabulary and only for the microcosm.

What, then, is left "outside our mind"? Recall that both Aristotle and Kant start their accounts with the conception of the external object as the efficient cause of our perceptions. The answer, of course, is that the external object still exists, but it has lost its pristine status. Neither Aristarchus nor Copernicus wanted to diminish the earth. They just wanted to exalt the sun. Aristotle says, "It is impossible that the subjects which cause our perception should not exist . . . necessarily prior to the perception" (*Metaphysics* 1010B). Kant says that "corresponding to the Sensibility viewed as receptivity . . . there is the transcendental object . . . the purely intelligible cause of appearances in general . . . which is given itself prior to all experience" (A494=B522).

A main job, according to Kant, of the new efficient cause intrinsic to the structure of our minds is to work up the raw material of sense impressions into knowledge of objects. Thus, even in the process of perception we are both passive and active. We passively sense or intuit sense data, but, as Aristotle's example indicates, "in taking this white datum for a man" we can run into error. If we can run into error, then there must be within us a principle that enables us to combine or synthesize the sense data so that we can make a wrong perception, "for falsehood always involves a synthesis" *(synthesei)* while "the principle which makes *(poiun)* the synthesis is in every case the mind" (18A, 30B). Aristotle does not say which mind does this, but the words "synthesis" and "makes" leave it beyond doubt. Kant, as we expect, has the same idea and uses much the same words: "works up," "synthesis," "makes," etc. Such, then, is a primary job of the active mind.

This brings me to the difficulty with Imagination, which for both men is initially a new and independent faculty. Is it passive or active? In Aristotle's case, clearly it is passive: I can excite images at pleasure and make my own scenery as I see fit. "This making of images lies in our power whenever we will" (27B). Moreover, we learn later that Imagination belongs to the primary sense faculty, that is, if I am right, to passive mind (50A), while the maker of images is, in my view, the same active mind as the one involved in perception.

Kant's complicated description amounts, I believe, to the same thing: "The Imagination is the faculty of representing in intuition an object that is not itself present. Now since all our intuition is sensible, the Imagination . . . belongs to Sensibility." Since the Sensibility is a passive faculty, the Imagination is, therefore, a passive faculty. Something must act upon it. Although the phrases "productive imagination" and "the transcendental synthesis of imagination" may suggest that Imagination itself is an agent, this suggestion is immediately corrected, for we learn that this synthesis is an action of the Understanding on the Sensibility," and that the Understanding, under the title of a transcendental synthesis of imagination performs this act upon the passive subject whose faculty it is" (B151-53).

What are the objects of thought? An important class of objects for both Aristotle and Kant is images. We think with images and of universals or concepts, and only images are in the mind. Aristotle holds that "the thinking faculty thinks the form in images. . . . It is impossible even to think without an image. The same affection is used in thinking as in using a diagram. . . . Although we may not be thinking of a finite size we still put a finite size before our eyes" (*On Memory* 49B–50A). Kant says: "We cannot think a line without drawing it in thought," that is, presumably, as an image in the passive mind or Sensibility; we cannot think of time "except under the image of a line which we draw"; and "we know our own subject only as appearance," that is, presumably, as an image in the Sensibility (B154, 156).

PASSIVE AND ACTIVE MINDS

Some striking differences between Aristotle and Kant are evident especially in their views of the roles played by the passive and active minds in regard to thinking. Because Aristotle holds that "thinking is a form of being acted upon," a passion *(paschein)*, a receiving (29A, 29B), he must hold that it is the passive mind that thinks, that thoughts are in it potentially, that it is the "receptacle" or "subject" of thoughts, images, and sensations. Passive mind is thus a substance in the sense of subject or substratum in which attributes inhere and out of which things are produced. Therefore, passive mind, could be properly called "Understanding." If this is true of passive mind, Aristotle must hold the paradoxical view that its partner, active mind, although it is called "mind," does not think at all. Its role is to activate the passive mind to think. Because it is an efficient cause, an unmoved mover, the source from which the whole series of movements in the process is derived, active mind could be appropriately called "Will" and given the status of a faculty. Berkeley, as we have noticed, does this. Obviously the products of the union of the Will and the Understanding are thoughts.

As we have noticed, Kant, like Aristotle, holds that the passive mind or Sensibility is receptive of or intuits sensations and images and that it is acted upon by the active mind. Moreover, again like Aristotle, Kant holds that the active mind is spontaneous, that is, an unmoved mover, an agent or maker, that acts upon the Sensibility to produce knowledge of objects. "Wherever there is action," he says, "and therefore activity and force, there is also substance; [and such] action signifies the relation of the subject of causality to its effect" (A204–205= B249–250). Kant's Understanding, like Aristotle's active mind, is an agent, a productive or generative power like Plato's divine Father or Craftsman.

How, then, does Kant differ from Aristotle? First, whereas Aristotle holds that thinking is a passion of the passive mind, Kant holds that thinking is the action of the active mind and that the Understanding thinks as an agent acts or causes.

Second, Kant ascribes to this active substance or causal agent passive characteristics by showing that the Understanding is a substratum, a thing standing under, not just in name *(Verstand)* but in content. He identifies the Understanding with the "I": ". . . In all our thought the 'I' is the subject in which thoughts inhere" (A349 = B406). This is true of the logical subject: "In it, therefore, as the transcendental subject, all our perceptions must be found." But it is true also of the ontological subject, "the real subject in which the thought inheres," for beyond the "logical meaning of the 'I,' "although admittedly we have no knowledge of it, there is "the subject in itself, which as substratum underlies this logical 'I,' as it does all thoughts" (A350). Thus in Kant's mind, the Understanding, in either its logical or ontological meaning, is a capacity to receive thoughts like Kant's own Sensibility, which receives impressions. In its passive role, Kant's Understanding and Aristotle's passive mind resemble the well-known archetype in Western thought of substratum and receptivity, Plato's Receptacle, "the Nurse of all Becoming."

On one occasion, in a well-known passage, Kant makes the Understanding both Agent and Patient: "Through this I or he or it (the thing) which thinks, nothing further is represented than a transcendental subject of thoughts = X" (A346 = B404). In the first part of the sentence, the thing that thinks is a causal agent; in the second part the subject of thoughts is a substratum or receptacle. Thus, from Aristotle's point of view, Kant fuses the two hemispheres of the mind.

Since the second self or "I" is not just "the constant logical subject of thought," the transcendental subject, but also the ontological subject, I conclude that Kant's talk of faculties is more than a way of talking, that the faculty is not reducible to the way it is manifested in its activities and objects, and that his faculty psychology is a revelation of his ontology. Kant gives us not just the logical but also the ontological geography of that enchanted island, the mind (cf. A235 = B294).

CONCLUSION: KANT'S MIND-CENTERED UNIVERSE

In making a theory of mind, Kant appears to satisfy one main feature of the Procreation Model better even than Aristotle in ancient times and more fully than any in modern times, including Berkeley. This main feature of the model, when transferred to the theory, is the active power to create. Kant's account is "better" than Aristotle's in that the latter does not spell out in any detail how his *nous poietikos* or active mind is actualized but leaves it to the reader to fill in the gaps. Perhaps some pages in the *De Anima* have been lost, for, as we have noticed, most recent commentators conclude that active mind has no real function. Kant, however, does furnish detail, and he does this "more fully" than Berkeley. Whereas, the latter gives us the principles whereby we create our worlds with "the mind active" by combining certain sense data to make stones, trees, books, etc., each of which is "a particular combination of ideas arbitrarily put together by the mind" (*Principles* 1, 12), he still leaves it to the reader to fill in the gaps. Kant, however, provides the reader with items that are written only between the lines, so to speak. As we have seen, "we ourselves introduce . . . the order and regularity in the appearances that we call *nature*" (A125). Just as Copernicus hypothesizes a sun-centered universe, Kant envisages a mind-centered universe of experience. Just as Plato uses the sun as a model for the Good who, like the Father of the *Timaeus,* is the creator of the Cosmos, so Kant, albeit indirectly, uses the sun as a model for the active mind.

While this treatment of the active mind constitutes an advance of the greatest importance in the history of theories of the mind, nevertheless, as it seems to me, we encounter a significant weakness in Kant's attempt to present his account in terms of the subject-inherence and subject-predicate conceptions. The Procreation Model tells us that the subjects of inherence and thus the substance as substratum are passive entities that lie under, support, and contain, as do the womb and the Receptacle of Plato's account. As we have now seen, however, Kant calls the active mind "Understanding" and treats it as a subject and substratum in which thoughts inhere. Perhaps Kant could have avoided this difficulty by adopting throughout his account the suggestions offered by the Procreation Model, thus fitting his theory to the pattern made by Plato and Aristotle instead of trying to fit it to more recent interpretations of the subject-predicate model.

Let us then retain the Procreation Model as a device for making a theory of mind that enables us to accommodate many of the generally agreed upon facts. But since theories of mind have suffered, in my view, by using subject-predicate and substance-attribute models, finding a new auxiliary model to Procreation that avoids the pitfalls of the subject-predicate, will be helpful. Such a model is the Reader-Writer. Here is a model rich in connotation, powerful and flexible in application, and familiar to all that has a chance of illuminating additional areas concerning the structure and workings of the mind.

CHAPTER 6

Finding an Auxiliary Model:
The Mind as Reader and Writer

In the mind of the infant we find the initial absence of substantive objects followed by the construction of solid and permanent objects.

Jean Piaget

In this chapter I reveal more about the structure and operations of the mind from a different point of view. We shall see that although the two hemispheres of the mind remain as secure as ever, they are described as receptive and active instead of passive and active, and both are present at the creation of a percept or a work of art. I also bring out some of the main ways in which the mind operates with symbols and signs, that is, with what might be called "artificial" signs and "natural" signs.

To do this I use a new model that is a most helpful auxiliary to the Procreation Model, for it enables me to capture items not caught or not stressed in our main model. For example, while the great beauty of the Procreation Model is its feature of team effort contributing to joint products, it fails to bring out the activity of the "passive" mind. This gap is filled by the model of reading and writing. Moreover, the model enables me to offer an alternative to the substance-attribute way first of seeing and then of perceiving the world. Finally, this model enables me to show not only how we make works of art, but also how we make our world.

Paul Kolers suggests a promising approach to study of the mind in his article "Bilingualism and Information Processing."[1] He first observes that since one of the principal activities of the human mind is the manipulation of symbols, an investigation of how we use symbols will yield insights into the workings of the mind. Then he proposes that an investigation of how a bilinguist uses two sets of symbols will teach us much about mental operations. He summarizes his investigation: "A person who can speak two languages has clearly mastered two sets of symbols. Experiments that cause the two sets to interact provide important clues to how the mind works."

What interests me here is Kolers' second suggestion. If he is right, however, the investigation can be conducted nearer home. Nearly all of us fail to realize what we accomplished at a very early age: A person who can read and write one language has clearly mastered two sets of symbols. An investigation of how the two sets interact should tell us much about the workings of the mind. The two main ways of using symbols are interpreting and manipulating them, and the prototypes of these operations are reading and writing. I suggest also that the workings of the mind will be revealed more fully by considering not only bilingual subjects (those who can already read and write), but also subjects who are striving to become bilingual. It will be helpful to conduct the investigation still nearer home by looking at some of the most rudimentary ways of acquiring a language. As we shall see, all of us have been mastering code-breaking and encoding skills from earliest infancy. Let us begin with the ancient question of vision.

THE PROBLEM

Any adequate solution must be able to accommodate two sorts of facts. It must be able to fit in the very ordinary facts of common sense: popular suppositions such as that sight gives us a direct intuition of physical objects, including their distances, sizes, shapes, positions, and movements. But it must also allow for the apparent misfits: those not-so-extraordinary facts connected with illusion; for without these the whole problem of vision would never have been posed. Macbeth saw a dagger before him but could not clutch it. We see a lake before us in the desert, but we dip our pannikins into sand. We see in the distance a small, round tower, but we climb a large, square building. We see a bent

Fig. 6.1. Illusion

The Mind as Reader and Writer

stick partly immersed in water, but we pull out a straight one. What, then, do we actually see? What explains our deception, and how do we avoid being deceived?

THE TRADITIONAL DOCTRINE: THE CAMERA MODEL

Such cases prompted many theorists to ask questions like "How can what we directly see be the same as the physical object if the latter remains fixed but the former varies?" Their answers persuaded them to reject the popular supposition that sight gives us a direct intuition of physical reality and to adopt the view that it gives us a direct intuition only of a copy or a picture of reality. This view, styled the Copy or the Representative theory, dominates our Western tradition. The hidden model for this view is the camera. Kepler, the father of modern optics and the inventor of the first portable camera obscura, specified its main features: The eye is a camera, a machine for taking photographs of physical objects. It is equipped with an aperture, a light-sensitive material, a converging lens, a focusing mechanism, and a screen on which the photograph is received.

Certainly the camera model brightly illuminates the dioptrics and structure of the eye. It shows the nature of clear and obscure, distinct and confused vision, and it exhibits the process of accommodation. But it sheds little light on how we see. We notice that the interpreter of the photographs is not built into the camera. To make it work we must sup-

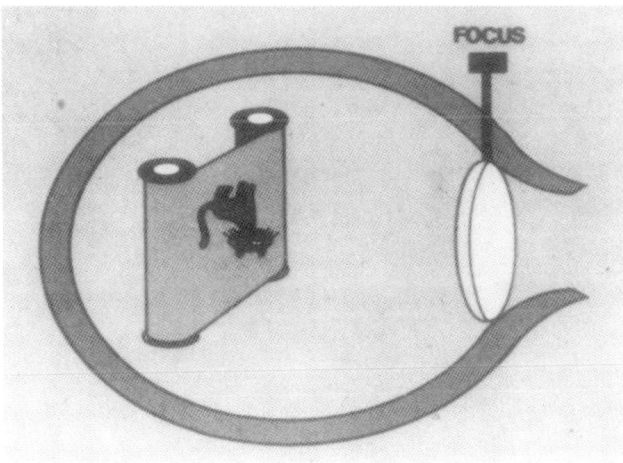

Fig. 6.2. The camera

pose a mind and another eye behind the camera, looking at and interpreting the photographs, just as Kepler had to get inside his own camera obscura. Accordingly, we are back where we started: How do we interpret the photographs or, indeed, any visual object? The obvious answer is that the photographs are pictures or copies of their originals. But then how do we tell whether the likenesses are good or bad when we cannot compare the pictures with their originals? We are forever confined to the contemplation of our own private photographs. Moreover, many photographs are most unlike the objects they are supposed to copy. Consequently, the camera model cannot suggest an adequate account of illusions. Indeed, it seems that the camera does a good job in creating them! The camera is notorious for such things as turning a maiden's minifeet into those of a mastodon.

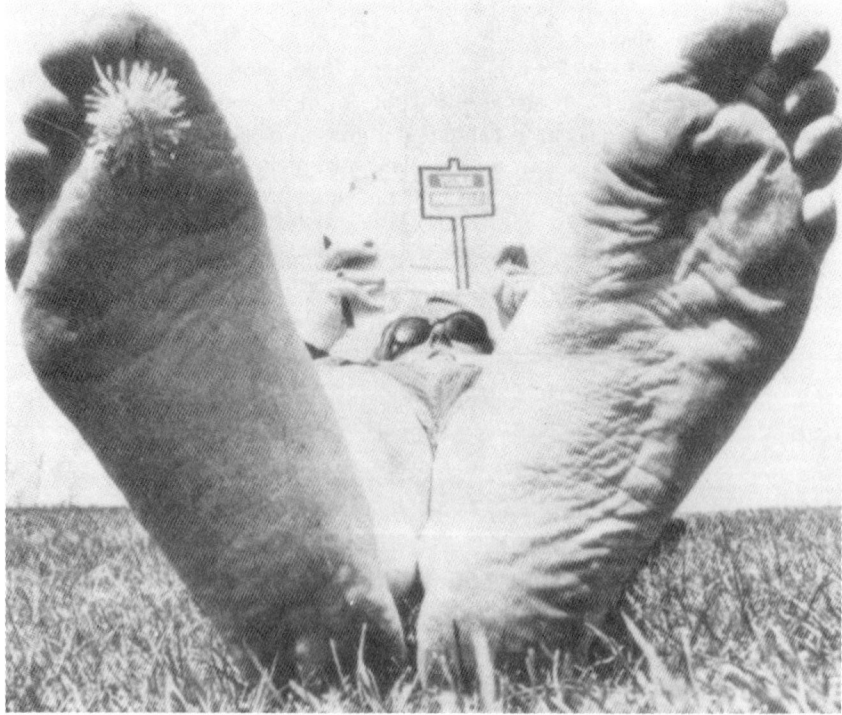

Fig. 6.3. Photographic distortion: James Laragy, Rochester, New York, courtesy of *Gannett* Newspapers

The Mind as Reader and Writer 99

The mind behind the camera may see the little upside-down pictures on the screen but cannot tell by sight that the originals are right side up. The mind may see the image of the crooked stick but cannot see that the stick is straight. The mind cannot tell which is bigger, the thumb or the Eiffel Tower and is even fooled by the images seen in the plane mirror. In all these cases the mind is deceived unless it is a mind with a memory and can interpret the pictures in the light of additional information, a mind who can tell and often mistell what things signify, and who, aware of contexts, can see through the ambiguities of vision. In short, it must be fooled unless it has learned to decode the complex code of vision, that is, to read the language of vision.

A RIVAL HYPOTHESIS: TO SEE IS TO READ

My hypothesis is roughly defined by a remark made by the sculptor Naum Gabo: "Lines, shapes, forms, color, and movement have a lan-

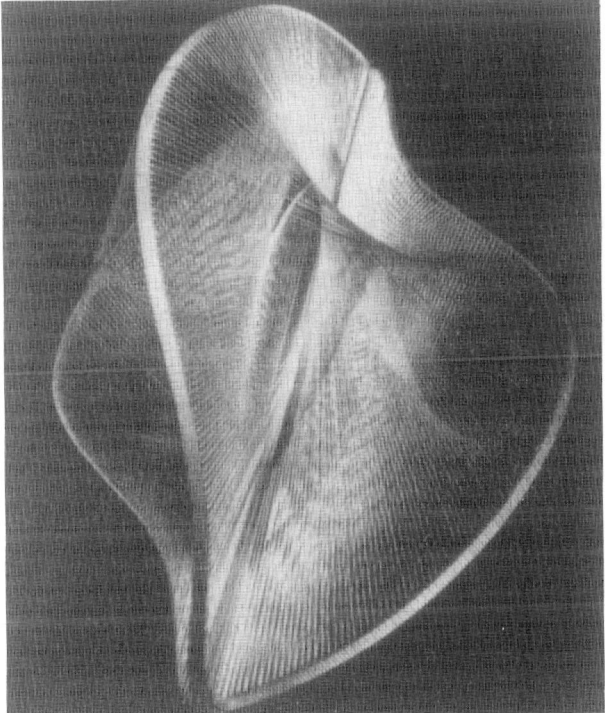

Fig. 6.4. Naum Gabo, *Linear Construction No. 2,* plastic

guage of their own, but reading takes time. It is not enough to look. You must see, and 'see' means 'read'." This hypothesis—that to see is to read a language whose elements are lines, shapes, forms, color, and movement—is a development of the ideas of two "philologists": Plato, who wrote shortly after the invention of the modern alphabet, and George Berkeley, who wrote shortly after the invention of modern optics. Berkeley presented the view that the visible world is a script in alphabetical form, which we have to learn to read. I shall develop this conception in order to suggest a solution to the ancient problem of how we see.[2]

DROPPING THE COPY THEORY: THE TWO LANGUAGES

Equipped with the view that visual objects constitute *a language*, I could proceed to interpret the words of this language as visual objects and their referents as physical objects, leaving it unspecified whether the words are those of a written or a spoken language. Visual objects would suggest, or function as signs of, physical objects, just as words suggest or signify their referents. By adopting this model I could deduce that physical objects are not objects directly or intuitively seen, for when we hear the word *apple,* there is no need to see an apple, only to think of it. This model has many merits.[3] By indicating a sharp distinction between the sign and the thing signified it suggests how we can accommodate illusions. Illusions are properly delusions; that is, we make mistakes not about things that are the gifts of sight, but only about what they prompt us to believe. But the model fails to suggest how we can accommodate common sense, according to which we directly see physical objects. We need a far more intimate relation than that between a word and its referent yet one that preserves their distinctness.

This desideratum is satisfied, it seems to me, by that peculiar relation between the items of the written and spoken languages of what we commonly call the same language. When as children we learn to read and write, our aim is to bridge the gap between these two different languages. It is strange that we now think them one language, for the gap between them is in some respects far wider than that between, for example, spoken English and spoken Italian or the hieroglyphs and the Greek script carved on the Rosetta stone. The elements of spoken and written languages belong to two different sense realms. Presented with the new and unknown written language, which we have to read in order to be admitted into the exclusive literate society, we are, in fact, confronted with a decoding problem of enormous complexity. However, we are al-

The Mind as Reader and Writer

Fig. 6.5. The two languages, spoken and written

ready equipped with a language that is old and known, namely, our own native but artificial tongue, the spoken language.

Let me narrow this interpretation. Instead of assuming merely that visual objects constitute a language, I assume that visual objects constitute *a written language*. More specifically, I interpret the letters of this written language as visual sizes, shapes, positions, and movements; and the letters of the corresponding *spoken language* as the spatial properties of physical objects, that is, their sizes, shapes, positions, and movements. These physical objects, I assume, could be known by us even if we had not been gifted with sight. This is not an implausible assumption, for it appears that blind people possess spatial awareness. Indeed, the people in H. G. Wells' "Country of the Blind" knew more about the spatial features of their world than did the sighted intruder. With this interpretation I can at once divorce myself from the most fundamental feature of the traditional Copy theory of vision. I deduce that visual objects—including photographs, paintings, and sculptures—are not copies or replicas of the objects they represent to us. This paradox is merely an easy application of an obvious feature of language. The written language, it is true, began with signs that were pictures, but it ended with alphabetical signs that are not. The hieroglyphs themselves nicely exemplify this paradox. Certainly the hieroglyphs look as if they are to be read pictorially or allegorically, and because of this they fooled the best philologists for more than two thousand years. There is little resemblance between a goose and a son, a vulture and a mother, or an owl and a crocodile, yet the sacred scribes used pictures of the former to represent the latter—not because the members of each pair were alike but because they were called by similar names. Thus I deduce that there is no more resemblance between visual sizes, shapes, and movements and their corresponding tactual sizes, shapes, and movements than there is between the letter A and the many phonemes it represents or between the marks CAT and the sound *kăt,* even though, outdoing the Egyptians, we call members of each pair by the same names.

How do I test this important theorem? It seems to me that if the letters and words of visual language are not replicas of what they represent, then a foreigner to this language cannot read it.

A primary sense of the verb *read,* according to the *Shorter Oxford English Dictionary,* is "to peruse and utter in speech," that is, "to translate from the written into the corresponding spoken language." This produces a tame and obvious truth in the terms of the model. It is easy to give a foreigner to the written language a reading test. We need someone who is familiar with the spoken language and a foreigner to the written—a child, for example, before he has learned his letters. Con-

Fig. 6.6. The owl and the crocodile, hieroglyph

fronted for the first time with specimens of the written language, such as the marks CAT, the illiterate proves quite unable to translate them into the spoken word kăt, although he knows this word intimately.

However, the *Oxford* definition produces a more exciting and not-so-obvious truth in the terms of my theory. It is not so easy to give a foreigner to visual language a reading test. We need someone new to vision and old to touch, for example, a congenitally blind person who is suddenly made to see. We can predict that such a visual illiterate, confronted visually for the first time with such objects as a cube and a sphere, will be unable to tell which is the cube and which is the sphere, although he knows both of them well by touch. This prediction, so it happens, turns out to be true. The test has been carried out on numerous occasions. None of the tests, it seems to me, disconfirms our theory. Three typical statements from the reports on these cases are as follows: "The patient is shown a sphere and a cube. . . . He realizes that the two are distinct, but does not know which is round and which cornered . . . "; "He could not in the least say which was the cube and which the sphere . . ."; "He remains absolutely incapable of saying whether it is round or cornered."[4] As one expects, these visual illiterates, confronted for the first time with those paradigms of the Picture theory (namely, photographs of familiar objects) have no idea how to read them. But unexpectedly, even visually literate persons who have not learned the code of photography (for example, Australian aborigines from the heart of the outback) can make nothing of photographs. Therefore, by dropping the Picture theory of language, we are able to drop the Picture theory of pictures.

LEARNING TO READ

If, however, we cannot have recourse to the Picture Theory, how do we bridge the gap between visuals and tactuals? Once more, an easy application of the written-spoken language model provides the answer. As children confronted with specimens of this mysterious writing, our aim is to break its code and become readers or native decoders, able to translate the foreign marks into sounds of spoken English. Our predicament is similar to that of Champollion when he began to decipher the hieroglyphs. Like him, we must transfer our knowledge of a language that is old and known to another that is new and unknown. Fortunately, to help us solve what is perhaps the second most difficult problem that we shall ever be called upon to face, we possess the all-important factor that Champollion lacked. We have a teacher who can teach us the letters and their proper names. These we learn by ostensive definition, the way we begin to learn any foreign language. This involves establishing an association between entirely different things so that when shown a letter or a word we can tell its spoken name. The process takes time and experience and repeated acts.

Parallel remarks apply to the beginning reader in visual language. Here is a student whose mastery of the letters of this new language is being tested. On the second day of testing, the once-blind man is shown a watch. " 'Is it round? Is it a round thing or a square one?' No answer. 'Do you know what a square is?' He positions his two hands to form a square. 'And a circle?' He again bends his hand to produce a ring. In looking at the watch at which his gaze is obviously directed, he remains absolutely incapable of saying whether it's round or cornered. However much I insist on an answer, none is forthcoming. On the following morning the same question, the same inability to answer. So I then let him feel the watch. No sooner has he taken it in his hand than he immediately says, 'That's round, it's a watch.' "[5] After countless repetitions the beginner can tell the names of the letters of visual language and some of its words.

The remaining items of visual language are learned in terms of the basic ones. A child who has learned his letters and a few basic terms can read words that are wholly new to him. For example, having read the word *bar*, he is well on the way to reading the new word *Barbarian*. Similarly, the learner of visual language, equipped with a knowledge of the visual analogues of round, square, straight, curved, etc., can guess, by looking, the names of wholly new objects. Eventually, with the help of analogies, he may even be able to see the moon and flying saucers although he has never handled these objects. He might even become as good a reader as Lady Macbeth when she said to her husband: "Your face, my thane, is as a book whereon men may read strange matters." She might have said: "Your intentions are written all over your face, but I alone can read your writing."

Unhappily, the code of visual language is chaotic. This introduces visual illusions and thus sets the problem of vision. In illusion, as the etymon suggests, we are played against or mocked. At times, being genuinely cheated or deceived, we lose the game; at others, having seen through the deception, we win. Rarely are such expert readers as we are now taken in for more than an instant, but, as theorists, we must try to become strange to the familiar. What explains illusion? Why are we deceived, and how do we avoid being deceived?

The Mind as Reader and Writer

The model of the two languages is rich in its offerings here. The child learning to read English is baffled not merely by an enormously complex code but by one that is crazy. He cannot readily overcome the disparity between the sounds of his mother tongue and the symbols he sees on the page. The English alphabet contains only 26 letters but over 80 sounds. Thus one character may be translated into many different phonemes. Nothing in the character *O* itself tells the child which translation to pick: the sound represented in *go, one, do, gone,* or *women.* Conversely, many different characters may translate into only one phoneme. There is nothing in the different characters present in *to, woo, flew, canoe,* and *rheumatism* that can tell the beginning reader to translate them into only one sound. Finally, how is the frustrated beginner to know that some characters, such as the *b* in *comb,* the *e* in *cause,* and the *h* in *herb* do not translate into sound at all (at least in American English)? It is easy to see why the young player loses these language games. Winning the game with the *f* in *aft, if,* and *oft,* he forthwith loses it with the *f* in *of.* Able to read the combinations *might, right, light,* and *tight,* the shocking truth is revealed when he encounters the combination *eight.*

The beginning reader in visual language is equally baffled. The explanation of his deception is much the same as that of the other reader. Finding that certain visual sizes, shapes, positions, etc., are regularly translated into their tactual counterparts, he expects this regularity to continue. Encountering cases that to us are no longer extraordinary, the beginner is unavoidably mistaken. Having successfully translated blurriness into near distance, he mistranslates when he sees the same blurriness produced by an object out of focus behind a magnifying glass. Although one visual "character" may translate in two different ways, nothing in the visual bentness itself tells him it is really straightness. Although two or more different visuals may translate in only one way, nothing in the double visual itself tells him there is only one object; nothing in the elliptical and various other shapes tells him it is only one circle. Some visuals do not translate into tactuals at all, but there is nothing in the mirror image itself to tell him there is nothing there, just as there was nothing in the visual dagger that enabled Macbeth to translate it as "a dagger of the mind." Mocked by the ambiguities and other irregularities of visual language, it is no wonder the once-blind man asked: "Which is the lying sense, feeling or seeing?"

In spite of these defects many of us learn to read. How, then, do we avoid being deceived? Unfortunately, we have no analogue to Sir James

Pitman's Initial Teaching Alphabet, that it, a relatively simple code that we can break before we tackle the more complex code of vision.[6] The Initial Teaching Alphabet is a simpler system than English, although it contains more primitives: Pitman has almost doubled the number of letters of its alphabet and tripled the number of vowels. Nevertheless, each letter translates into only one phoneme of our old language. Thus the defects of our present alphabet (listed above) have been eliminated.

Fortunately, there are other devices to help in counteracting the capriciousness inherent in written or visual language. We rely upon two factors of great value, namely, our prenotions and context. In reading the written language, for example, we tend to overlook the typographical sizes and shapes and pass on to the translation: Since the sizes of the marks big and LITTLE are not especially relevant to the translation, we ignore them. This factor parallels the well-known size constancy of visual language. Thus although the visual size of an object halves as its distance from the eye doubles, the mind ignores such information and relies instead on more massive cues such as its prenotions of the size of the object. A man, for example, looks just as big at a hundred yards as at fifty. Indeed, the feat of returning to the old "innocence of the eye," built into the camera and prized by the Renaissance painters, requires an effort of attending or a glance through a grid.

The context of the characters on the page, or of the visual objects we seek to interpret, supplements this factor. Nothing in the combination READ, abstracted from its context, enables us to choose between the translation *rēd* and *rĕd*. Nevertheless, we translate successfully when it is preceded by such marks as TO or HAD. This illustrates how we avoid being deceived by many illusions; we can see that the stick, crooked in the context of air and water, is really straight. The example also illustrates how we put a stop to the ambiguities in some amusing figures and pictures. The small square in the diagram appears to flap in and out; what was a duck turns into a rabbit. The interpretations are fixed for us, however, when we are given additional cues: when figures of appropriate sizes are inserted in the squares; and when the duck's body is added.

WORD MAGIC

In the preceding account I showed first the nature of the gap between the visual and the tactual realms, then how, with the help of experience, we begin to bridge the gap. This is insufficient, however, for most people do not think there is any gap to bridge. We ordinarily say and believe that we see the same sizes, shapes, and positions that we feel. How, then, can one accommodate these popular suppositions?

The Mind as Reader and Writer

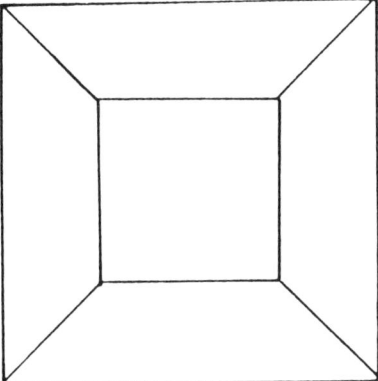

Fig. 6.7. The squares

Customarily, we call by the same name a word of the written language and the corresponding word in the spoken language, such as, for example, the marks SQUARE and the sound *skwăr*. We do the same with characters and phonemes, using, for example, the name "Double-U" not only for the mark W but for the sound into which it translates. The same custom is carried out with the specifically distinct sizes, shapes, positions, and movements of the visual and tactual realms. We use, for example, the same word *round* to refer to the shape of a watch that we see and to the shape that we feel.

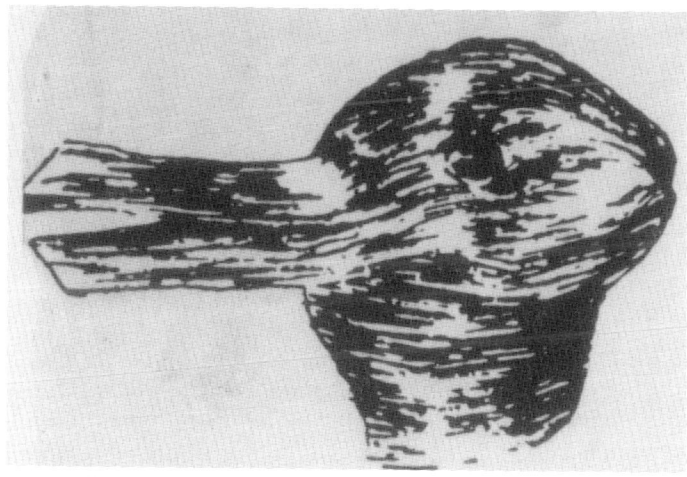

Fig. 6.8. The duck-rabbit

This custom is highly convenient. It saves an endless number of new words, and it constitutes a translation link—a Rosetta stone, as it were—between the members of each pair of languages. Although highly convenient, this custom leads us into error. There is a strong temptation to think that because we call them by the same names, the roundness, squareness, etc., that we see are the same roundness, squareness, etc., that we feel. Even though the correlations between written and spoken English were not learned in earliest infancy, we now not only call these two languages "one language," namely, "English," but we also think of them as one. The correlations between sight and touch were sucked in with our milk and the metalanguage established shortly thereafter. In this way visuals and tactuals are complicated, twisted together, knotted, or concreted together. The products of such confusions or complications of the items of the visual and the haptic realms constitute our visible world.

WRITING IN ORDINARY AND VISUAL LANGUAGE

If seeing is appropriately modeled upon reading, then painting, drawing, sculpture, and photography are appropriately modeled upon writing. All these arts, then, are forms of writing in visual language, though each has its own special medium, its own vocabulary and code.[7] The analogy between writing *(graphé)* and painting *(zographia)*, as well

Fig. 6.9. Thoth, Egyptian god of writing, Kestner Museum, Hanover

The Mind as Reader and Writer 109

as between drawing and sculpture, was noted by Plato. Furthermore, Plato treated all these arts as forms of handicraft *(cheiourgía)*. Finally, he used the legend of Thoth, the great inventor of writing, whom the Greeks called Hermes,[8] to make an important point: "What you have discovered is a recipe not for memory, but for reminder."[9] What we are reminded of when we read the written discourse is the "real" thing, the spoken discourse.

Writing, then, in terms of the model, is the manipulation of letters or other conventional characters to represent and remind a reader of items in the spoken language. A concrete symbol for this basic operation that we perform upon the spoken language is the "Seated Scribe." The

Fig. 6.10. Seated Scribe, Musée de Louvre, Paris

Scribe is taking dictation. Receiving a message in the primary language, he is in the process of translating it into another. Receiving, for example, the message *miseh* in plain text, he encodes it into the cryptograms of the owl, the bolt, and the twisted flax and, according to the rules of syntax, puts them together in order in an invisible rectangle to make a well-formed formula. Thus he bridges the enormous gap between the two languages in the reverse direction from reading, so that another reader can be reminded of the original. The bridge or translation link that he uses is spelling, which, like scaffolding, is dispensable. He bridges the gap by spelling the names of the items of the message, for these names constitute a rebus: they sound like the names of the vocabulary of the secondary language, the letters of his alphabet, which he has already learned by ostensive definition. It is, of course, accidental that the words of his metalanguage are in the same language as the original message. The characters and their syntax are conventional, based upon a compact between him and his reader. Otherwise they could not be decoded, and there could be no language. Nevertheless, within these conventions, he has his own unconventional writing style. Appropriately interpreted, this model illuminates how we write with visuals.

A simple form of writing is represented by the Australian aborigine who writes his message by breaking a twig and thus informs his readers of the presence of an old-man kangaroo. Lord Nelson sent a love note to Lady Hamilton by hoisting a flag. Samuel Butler, in his "Thought and Language," used the case of Mrs. Bentley to illustrate the same simple form. Mrs. Bentley used to send her snuffbox instead of an ordinary written order, to the college buttery at Trinity College when she wanted beer, and the butler was able to read her extraordinary writing just as readily in this style as in the other. This example satisfies the main features of the model. Observe that the convention or mutual compact necessary for language, was made between only one writer and one reader, even though the author chose to encode in an unconventional type of cryptogram designed to conceal the very existence of the message from any prying readers.

Although the camera model may not illuminate how we read visual language, the camera itself is a wonderful instrument for writing in it. The cryptograms into which we encode our messages from the visible world with this instrument are more readily decoded than typewritten or handwritten characters. An important feature about the photograph that we learned from our model is that it no more copies the visible world than the hieroglyph does its referent, and yet, again like the hieroglyph,

The Mind as Reader and Writer 111

it appears to do so. What explains this appearance? With the help of the model, I concluded that the things we see are complications or concretions of visual and haptic items. We have long since bridged the gap between the two realms and, through our prenotions and awareness of context, put a stop to ambiguity.

The striking feature of the camera is that without any help from the photographer, it uncomplicates the complex that is our visible world. It achieves this by translating a three-dimensional view of the world into cryptograms of color on a flat surface. If there were colored pictures on our retinas, and if we could see them, they would be photographs, because the camera and the eye (which, as we have seen, is just another camera) give us perspective. In my view, this should be the interpretation of the phrase "the innocence of the eye."

In perspective, to adopt Berkeley's definition, we suppose that we are looking through a gridded window at the world: "The eye sees all the parts and objects in the horizontal plane through certain corresponding

Fig. 6.11. Dürer, *Reclining Nude,* Staatliche Museen, Berlin

squares of the perpendicular diaphanous plane."[10] The objects in the horizontal plane represent our visible world, while the images projected on the perpendicular plane represent a viewer's visual window (the word *field* is inappropriate) or what the camera "sees." The latter is no copy of the former, for what is projected as relatively large may translate into something very small; conversely, what is seen by the camera as high up may be seen by the eye as only far away, and so on. Thus, though the photograph may not copy our visible world, it does copy our visual window. While it does not imitate what we see, it does imitate what we "see."

What distinguishes painting and drawing, those more complex forms of writing in visual language, from photography? What techniques or rules of syntax does the artist follow in order to transmit his message? If he does not copy the visible world, does he then draw the images on his visual window? There is little doubt that since the Renaissance this has been the leading idea of most painters. It is as if the inventors of perspective drawing had invented the idea of writing with the camera. It would be a mistake to think, however, that perspective is purely geometrical. The painter can project on his canvas two pictures equally large yet, by making one fainter and higher up, enable his readers to translate it as something a hundred times larger. In this he follows the rules of perspective, as does the camera. But does he have to do so?

The camera, writing according to fixed rules of syntax, is placed in an uncompromising position with regard to perspective. Just as it is very possible to write improperly through too strict an observance of grammar, so the camera (and some painters), governed by the rules of perspective, can run into mistakes. The skillful artist, however, not so tightly bound, can make a compromise with perspective and yet succeed in getting his message across to the reader. This begins to answer the puzzling question of why a painting can be more "true to life" or more "convincing" than a photograph. To us and to the artist, equipped with a mind as well as an eye, a man looks just as big at a hundred yards as another at fifty, but the camera, fooled by its built-in perspective, "sees" and describes him as twice as small. The artist, however, can pick and choose. If he paints the man as he looks, the viewer reads him as a giant. If he matches the photograph, the viewer reads him as a midget. Accordingly, he chooses the way of understatement with respect to visual size, perhaps underscoring faintness and situation on his canvas, and thereby produces a convincing reading.

What distinguishes painting from photography, then, is its flexibility or freedom from convention. Just as the writer can break some but

The Mind as Reader and Writer 113

not all rules of grammar, so the artist, such as the Egyptian scribe, Botticelli, or Chagall, can ignore the rules of perspective: While he is not free from all conventions (otherwise, his work could not be read), such unconventionality and other idiosyncrasies constitute his style or, as the etymon indicates, manner of writing.

An apparently simple but highly complex form of writing with visuals is sculpture, the art of carving figures in relief, in intaglio, or in the round. Because of the medium, with three dimensions built into it, the sculptor more than other artists appears to represent a three-dimensional subject by making a copy of it. If I am right, however, the sculptor no more makes a copy or replica of his subject than does the scribe who encodes the spoken message into painted characters on a flat surface or the photographer who takes a photograph of a statue.

It may be granted that my thesis can accommodate well-known symbolic compositions of the sculptor such as Picasso's bronze *Head of a Woman* (1932). Just as the obvious reading of the hieroglyph I have been using is an owl, a bolt, and twisted flax (cf. the once-obvious reading of the letter A as a bull's head) and the correct reading is the phonetic sequence *miseh* and, through it, a crocodile, so the obvious reading of Picasso's composition is a smiling face with hard, prominent nose and deeply modeled mouth, whereas the "correct" reading is a happy blending of the male and female sex organs and, through it, the conception of the mutual subjectivity of sexual intercourse. (This is to accept John Berger's illuminating account of the work in which "its secret is a metaphor.")[11] Although I present the sequence from the reader's standpoint, one has only to reverse it to obtain the writer's sequence from the conception to the set of cryptograms. Unlike the scribe, Picasso has to invent his metaphor.

It may not be granted, however, that my thesis can accommodate those better known and apparently less symbolic compositions of the sculptor such as *Winged Victory of Samothrace*. The reader of this work is impressed by its naturalness. We see the Nike looking as if she were alive. We see what looks like soft cloth and the living flesh of her belly beneath the transparent drapery. However, all this is reader's talk after the artist has worked his magic upon us. We are talking about a magician's sleight of hand. Because it seems like living flesh we erroneously conclude that the artist tried to copy living flesh as he worked. In fact, with his reader in mind, this has been the artist's purpose. By his translation he has created the illusion of resemblance to cloth and flesh, just as the Wizard of Oz created the illusion in Dorothy's mind that Emerald

Fig. 6.12. Pablo Picasso, *Head of a Woman,* 1932, bronze, Museum of Modern Art, New York

Fig. 6.13. Winged Victory of Samothrace, fourth century B.C., Musée de Louvre, Paris

City was really green, or just as a genius, by inventing a metaphor, can create the resemblance between all the world and a stage or between a political boundary and an iron curtain. All this is clinched for me by the Nike's most striking feature: She seems to move with astonishing lightness and grace. Yet this heavy block of marble has been stationary on its pedestal in the Louvre for decades.

CONCLUSION:
HOW WE MAKE OUR WORLDS

These basic operations of reading and writing, appropriately interpreted, should be manifested in our cognitive operations at all age levels, even including the level of the neonate and the infant, that is, prior to the time in which we learn to read in the ordinary sense of the word. The importance of education at this level, long since stressed by educators, is slowly being realized by parents, for a single day of learning in the life of an infant is probably more valuable than a whole year at elementary school.

The model of reading and writing enabled us to discern some of the ways in which the mind works in seeing the world and in making works of art. Let me use the same model to elicit how our minds operate not just in seeing but in the early stages of perceiving. We return then, to our first lessons in learning to read, in other words, to the time when, somewhat familiar with much of our mother tongue, we are confronted with the foreign written language. Here I make use of the classic method of learning to read used by Plato, Berkeley, and many of us in this century including the author. Our teacher, having taught us our letters so that we can tell their names in our mother tongue, gives us our second lesson. She introduces us to the convention of substituting one complex term called *word* for the many simpler terms or proper names of the letters when the latter occur in a certain order. As three- or four-year-olds we are at first puzzled by these two lessons and ask why we cannot read (aloud) **ăpl** or **woch** straight off instead of having to say first **ā pē pē el ē** or **dubl yōō ´ā tē cē āch**. Why must we learn the names of the letters at all? We remain puzzled until we learn that knowing how to spell the names of the letters helps us to bridge the gap between the two languages. This is true of ancient Greek and modern Italian in which the sounds of the names of the letters are acrophonetic, that is, they are repeated in the sounds of the letters themselves. Regrettably, however, it is not true of English with its 26 letters and 80 sounds.

Although we master the skill of reading long after infancy, let me apply the model to the task of the infant in order to discover how he

The Mind as Reader and Writer

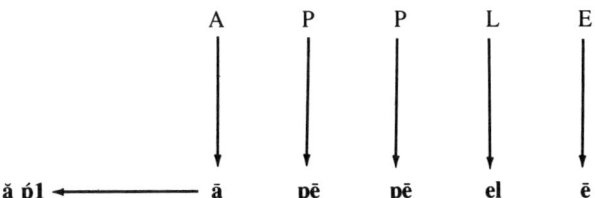

Fig. 6.14. Second lesson in reading

constructs his world. This requires a wider interpretation of the letters of our model. Instead of reading them only as visuals such as lines, shapes, forms, color, and movement (as Gabo prescribed), I interpret them as the sensible qualities of all the senses: some of them as sounds of various kinds, some as tastes, others as smells, and still others as tactuals. The letters of this alphabet of nature will, of course, be more numerous than the elements or letters of Euclid and of chemistry, but because they repeat themselves endlessly, they will remain relatively few. We see at once that these first two lessons of our model illustrate more vividly than does the Procreation Model the two stages of perception distinguished by the four theorists whose work I have described in this book. These theorists were unanimous in isolating the given in perception, that is the sensa or sense data (so-called because the mind is thought to be passive in receiving them). But none speaks with a clear voice on the second stage of perception to which the model points. Aristotle and Kant, using or reflecting the use of the Procreation Model, clearly indicate that the percept (for example, an apple or a watch) is a joint product of something outside us and our minds. But the Reading Model in its role as an auxiliary to procreation offers a feature that is missing in the latter. It shows more clearly than does the Procreation Model how the mind synthesizes outside data.

The sensible qualities in the language of nature that we have to read are not laid out for us as neatly as the English letters shown above in which there are already gaps between groups. They are more like the written Greek that Plato read, in which there are no gaps, no periods, no lowercase letters, and therefore no words in the text until Plato "read them into it." This models what we did as infants in reading the book of nature. The procedure is described by Berkeley: "As several of these [sensible qualities] are observed to accompany each other, they come to be marked by one name, and so to be reputed as one thing. Thus, for example, a certain color, taste, smell, figure and consistence having

WECANNOTLIVEWITHOUTLAWS

Fig. 6.15. Sentence from the Book of Nature

been observed to go together, are accounted one distinct thing signified by the name 'apple' " (*Principles* 1). This gives some idea of our enormous accomplishment as infants in reading the foreign language of nature, or our embellishment of the basic furniture of the earth. The language of nature does not come with any of its "words" formed for us. The power of our active minds is such that when we "see" particular things or physical objects we are makers or poets.

Much of this is confirmed by Jean Piaget. The mind of the infant, if we accept Piaget's own investigations, is never passively receiving but always acting. For example, the infant, finding no permanent things or substances, has to make them. Piaget refers to "the initial absence of substantive objects, followed by the construction of solid and permanent objects," and, by the end of the second year, to the synthesizing of the different visual, tactual, oral, etc., spaces into one space."[12] All this reflects the ways in which we learn to read by combining many letters into one word and accounting them one entity.

It suggests to me also a way of viewing the world that is different from the view presented in the first chapter of this book, namely, the way of subject-predicate and substance-attribute, so deeply entrenched in our conceptual scheme, which holds that the world consists of substances and their attributes and language of subjects and their predicates. This view assumes that as infants we find substances or physical objects in the world and learn to attach attributes to them; whereas, in the reader-writer view, we learn to make or construct these entities by painstaking trial and error from "qualities." Put in terms of language, in one way there are subjects and predicates joined by the copula or the *is* of predication, while in the other there are definienda and definientes joined by the *is* of identity. In the latter view, just as the child adds nothing to the combination of letters by calling these letters by one name, so the infant adds nothing to his world by making these so-called substances out of the qualities he experiences.

Notes

INTRODUCTION

1. Gilbert Ryle, *The Concept of Mind* (London: Hutchinson's University Library, 1949), pp. 1, 16.
2. Colin M. Turbayne, *The Myth of Metaphor* (Columbia: University of South Carolina Press, 1970), p. 12. First edition, New Haven: Yale University Press, 1962. This definition is much the same as Ryle's definition of "category mistake" just given. From the standpoint of metaphor a category mistake would be to take a metaphor literally, whereas from the other standpoint, a metaphor would be an intentional category mistake.

CHAPTER 1

1. Thomas Reid, *Essays on the Intellectual Powers of Man* (Edinburgh: 1785), VI, 6, 6.
2. Bertrand Russell, "On the Relations of Universals and Particulars," in *Logic and Knowledge*, ed. R. C. Marsh (London: Allen and Unwin, 1956), pp. 105, 123.
3. P.F. Strawson, *Individuals* (London: Methuen, 1959), ch. 6.
4. *Third set of Objections* II. For Descartes, inherence and predication amount to the same thing. "When we say that any attribute is contained in the nature or concept of anything, that is precisely the same as saying that it is true of that thing or can be affirmed of it." "Arguments Drawn up in Geometrical Fashion," Definition IX.
5. Boswell remarks: "I observed [to Dr. Johnson] that though we are satisfied Berkeley's doctrine is not true, it is impossible to refute it. I never shall forget the alacrity with which Johnson answered, striking his foot with mighty force against a large stone, till he rebounded from it, 'I refute it thus'." James Boswell, *The Life of Samuel Johnson*, 1791 Globe (London: Macmillan, 1929), p. 162.
6. See David Hume, *A Treatise of Human Nature* (London, 1739), Appendix.
7. *Individuals*, p. 88.
8. See F. P. Ramsey, "Universals" (1925), in *The Foundations of Mathematics* (London, 1931), ch. 4.
9. See *The Myth of Metaphor*, ch. 1.
10. "The Philosophy of Logical Atomism," 1918, in Marsh, p. 205.
11. *Individuals*, ch. 3.

CHAPTER 2

1. A. E. Taylor, *Plato: The Man and His Work*, sixth ed. (New York: Meridian Books, Inc., 1956), p. 460, and A. E. Taylor, *A Commentary on Plato's Timaeus* (Oxford: Clarendon Press, 1928), p. 635.
2. F. M. Cornford, *Plato's Cosmology* (Indianapolis and New York: The Bobbs-Merrill Co. Inc., 1957), p. 357 n. The word "appendix" is Cornford's, p. 355.
3. See W. H. S. Jones in his introduction to his translation of *Hippocrates*, vol. IV (Cambridge: Harvard University Press, 1967), pp. ix, x.
4. "The Nature of Philosophical Problems and Their Roots in Science," *British Journal for the Philosophy of Science*, vol. III (1952), p. 152.
5. This definition accords with the view of metaphor I developed in *The Myth of Metaphor*.
6. G. E. L. Owen, in "The Place of the *Timaeus* in Plato's Dialogues," *Classical Quarterly*, New Series, vol. III (1953), pp. 79–95, argues convincingly for the view that the *Timaeus*, like the *Republic*, is a middle dialogue, whereas H. F. Cherniss in his "Relation of the *Timaeus* to Plato's Later Dialogues," *American Journal of Philology*, vol. 78, (1957), pp. 225–60, argues for the traditional view that the *Timaeus* is a late dialogue.
7. Julian Marias, "Philosophic Truth and the Metaphoric System," in *Interpretation: The Poetry of Meaning*, ed. Stanley Romaine Hopper and David L. Miller (New York: Harcourt, Brace & World, Inc., 1967), p. 46.
8. Gilbert Ryle, in his *Plato's Progress* (Cambridge: Cambridge University Press, 1966), p. 14, approaches this view. He writes, "The Plato who compiled what is in large part a textbook for medical students . . ."
9. *Platonis Timaeus interprete Chalcidio cum eiusdem commentario*, ed. J. Wrobel (Leipsig, 1876). See also Raymond Klibansky, *The Continuity of the Platonic Tradition* (London: The Warburg Institute, 1939), pp. 26, 28.
10. Kilbansky, p. 35, and Plate 1 from British Museum, Ms. Cotton Vitellius [III].
11. Gregory Vlastos, in his *Plato's Universe* (Seattle: University of Washington Press, 1975), p. 26, admits that the Father image is invoked in the *Timaeus* but claims that it is "marginal," that the "associations of paternity are not followed out in the creation story . . . but only those prompted by the Craftsman metaphor," and that "phrases like 'contriving,' 'moulding,' . . . carry the bulk of the narrative." In his own account, however, Vlastos himself follows out the "associations of paternity" by referring not to the "contriving" of the cosmos by the Craftsman, but to its "creation." The word "creation" (Latin) or, better, its Greek counterpart "generation" *(genesis)*, is not only part of the primary vocabulary of the Father metaphor; it recurs throughout the *Timaeus* and conjures up the main image of the dialogue.

12. See Ilza Veith, *Hysteria: The History of the Disease* (Chicago: University of Chicago Press, 1965), pp. 10ff.
13. *Plato's Cosmology*, p. 181.
14. R.B. Onians, *The Origins of European Thought* (Cambridge: Cambridge University Press, 1951), p. 122.
15. This fits with the notion of *eros* in the *Symposium* and with the claim in the *Republic* that desire exists in every part of the soul. Both of these are middle dialogues.
16. Herman Weyl, *Symmetry* (Princeton: Princeton University Press, 1952), reprinted in part in *The World of Mathematics*, ed. James R. Newman (New York: Simon and Schuster, 1956), vol. I, p. 719.
17. Albert Einstein, "The Problem of Space, Ether, and the Field in Physics," in *Essays in Science* (New York: Philosophical Library Inc., 1934), p. 32.
18. The reading *poietou*, that of the ninth-century Codex Parisiensis A, is accepted by R. D. Archer-Hind, *The Timaeus of Plato* (London: Macmillan, 1888), reprinted (New York: Arno Press, 1973), p. 344. It is rejected by Taylor (pp. 646ff.) and Cornford (p. 349) in favor of *noetou*.
19. T.S. Eliot, for example, at the end of *The Waste Land* (New York: Harcourt Brace Jovanovich, 1971), p. 147, provides a key to "the plan and a good deal of the incidental symbolism of the poem."

CHAPTER 3

1. Unless stated otherwise, all references in this chapter are to the *De Anima* using, for example, 31A instead of 431A. Abbreviation for the *Generation of Animals* is *GA*. Following W. D. Ross, *Aristotle: De Anima* (Oxford: Clarendon Press, 1961), I have omitted, just before the last sentence, the words: "Actual knowledge is identical with its object: but potential knowledge is prior in time in the individual, but not prior in time in general." These words recur in ch. 7, 31A 1-3, where they properly belong.
2. J. H. Randall, *Aristotle* (New York: Columbia University Press, 1960), p. 102.
3. See, for example, A. L. Peck, *Aristotle: Generation of Animals* (London: Heinemann, 1942; Cambridge: Harvard University Press, Loeb Classical Library, 1963), Preface; J. H. Randall, *Aristotle*, pp. 126, 220-24; and A. Preus, *Science and Philosophy in Aristotle's Biological Works* (Hildesheim: Georg Olms, 1975), p. 1.
4. See, for example, Peck, pp. vi, vii, and Randall, p. 223. D. W. Hamlyn, *Aristotle's De Anima* (Oxford: Clarendon Press, 1968), p. ix, says that "in many sections the emphasis is definitely biological."
5. See *The Myth of Metaphor*, chapters 1 and 2.
6. See chapter 2 of this book.

7. Cf. Ross's translation: "By an incidental object of perception is meant such a fact as that the white object before us is the son of Diares; we perceive this *per accidens* because it is incidental to the white object which we perceive; that is why the perceiver is in this case not modified by the object of perception as such,"*Aristotle: De Anima*, p. 238. My translation derives some support from the paraphrase of Themistius (fourth century) quoted by R. D. Hicks, *Aristotle: De Anima* (Cambridge: Cambridge University Press, 1907), p. 363: "*Aristoteles de ta kata symbebekos aistheta houtos hermeneuei: kata symbebekos gar toutou aisthanetai, dioti to leuko hou aisthanetai touto symbebeken, hosper an eilegoi hoti kata symbebekos tou Diarous aisthanetai, hoti to leuko symbebeke Diarei einai.*" This may be translated: "Aristotle interprets incidental perception thus: This is perceived incidentally, because this is incidental to the white which is perceived, just as if one were to say that Diares is perceived incidentally, because it is incidental to the white to be Diares."

8. This applies also to Aristotle's other apparent example of an indirect object of perception, namely, the son of Cleon at 25A 25–27. If Diares, and not his son, is the indirect object, it is likely that Cleon, not the son of Cleon, is the indirect object, even though the text as it now stands does not lend itself to this interpretation. My view, however, is further supported by a later reference to Cleon at 30B 5; which is: "Cleon is white," not: "The son of Cleon is white."

9. G. E. Moore, "Refutation of Idealism," *Mind*, XII, no. 48 (October 1903). Reprinted in *Philosophical Studies* (London: Routledge and Kegan Paul, 1922), p. 18.

10. Bertrand Russell, *The Problems of Philosophy* (London: Home University Library, 1912). (New York: Oxford University Press, 1959), p. 42.

11. I have translated *energeia* in one case as "actuality" and in the other as "activity" primarily in order to avoid ascribing the notion of agency to a passive receptivity.

12. Bertrand Russell, *Analysis of Mind* (London: Allen & Unwin, 1921), p. 142.

13. Charles Kahn, in his "Sensation and Consciousness in Aristotle's Psychology," *Archiv Fur Geschichte Der Philosophie*, 48, 1 (1966), pp. 43–81, claims that the *De Anima* and *Parva Naturalia* are in "essential agreement" although the latter is "a definite advance" (p. 51). I am indebted to Kahn's study, especially his treatment of *sensus communis*.

14. See Ross, pp. 42–43, and Randall, pp. 100–01.

15. See, for example, Ross, pp. 45–47; Hicks, p. 503; and Hamlyn, p. 141.

16. Ross, pp. 44, 296.

17. See W. D. Ross, *Aristotle* (New York: Meridian Books, Inc.), pp. 40–50.

CHAPTER 4

1. Willis Doney, "Is Berkeley's a Cartesian Mind?" in *Berkeley: Critical and Interpretive Essays*, ed. C. M. Turbayne, (Minneapolis: University of Minnesota Press, 1982), pp. 273–82.

2. Citations from Berkeley's *A Treatise Concerning the Principles of Human Knowledge, Three Dialogues Between Hylas and Philonous*, and *Philosophical Correspondence Between Berkeley and Samuel Johnson* are from *Principles, Dialogues and Correspondence*, ed. C. M. Turbayne, (Indianapolis: Bobbs-Merrill, 1965, New York: Macmillan, 1984). Some words I have italicized for emphasis. References are by section numbers. In my edition I have sectioned the *Dialogues* in conformity with Berkeley's other works.

3. Cf. the first words of *Principles*, sect. 1, "It is evident to anyone . . . ," and his references in sect. 34 to "the principles hitherto *laid down*" and to "the principles *premised*."

4. For the names "Distinction Principle" and "Identity Principle," I am indebted to S. A. Grave, "The Mind and Its Ideas: Some Problems in the Interpretation of Berkeley," in *Locke and Berkeley, A Collection of Critical Essays*, ed. C. B. Martin and D. M. Armstrong, (New York: Doubleday, 1968), p. 298.

5. A. A. Luce, *Berkeley's Immaterialism* (London: Thomas Nelson and Sons, 1946), p. 51.

6. Edwin B. Allaire, "Berkeley's Idealism," *Theoria* 29 (1963): 229, 231; and "Berkeley's Idealism Revisited," *Berkeley: Critical and Interpretive Essays*, ed. C. M. Turbayne, pp. 197–206. Other recent contributors are R. Watson, "The Breakdown of Cartesian Metaphysics," *Journal of the History of Philosophy* 1, 2 (1963): 177–97; Phillip Cummins, "Perceptual Relativity and Ideas in the Mind," *Philosophy and Phenomenological Research* 24 (1963): 202–14; Harry M. Bracken, "Substance in Berkeley," in *New Studies in Berkeley's Philosophy*, ed. Warren E. Steinkraus (New York: Holt, Rinehart and Winston, 1966), pp. 85–97; L. N. Oaklander, "The Inherence Interpretation of Berkeley: A Critique," *Modern Schoolman* 54 (1977): 261–69; and George S. Pappas, "Ideas, Minds, and Berkeley," *American Philosophical Quarterly* 17, 3 (1980): 181–94.

7. G. E. Moore, "The Refutation of Idealism," in *Berkeley: Principles, Text and Critical Essays*, ed. C. M. Turbayne, (Indianapolis: Bobbs-Merrill, 1970), pp. 57–84. Originally published in *Mind* 12, 48 (1903): 433–53.

8. Grave, "Mind and Its Ideas," p. 298.

9. George Pitcher, *Berkeley* (London: Routledge and Kegan Paul, 1977), pp. 192–201.

10. A. J. Ayer, *Language, Truth and Logic* (1936; reprint New York: Dover, 1946), p. 126.

11. David Hume, *A Treatise of Human Nature* (London, 1739), bk. I, pt. IV, sect. 6.
12. Moore, "Refutation of Idealism," p. 73. Moore's "most famous criticism" and rejoinders by C. J. Ducasse and E. E. Harris are illuminatingly discussed by Steinkraus, "Berkeley and His Modern Critics," in his *New Studies*, pp. 159–62.
13. Bertrand Russell, *Problems of Philosophy* (New York: Oxford University Press, 1959), p. 42.
14. Bertrand Russell, *Analysis of Mind* (London: Allen and Unwin, 1921), p. 142.
15. P. A. Schilpp, ed., *The Philosophy of G. E. Moore* (Evanston: Library of Living Philosophers, 1942), p. 653.
16. Gilbert Ryle, *Concept of Mind* (London: Hutchinson, 1949), pp. 168–98.
17. See Robert Blanché, *Axiomatics* (London: Routledge and Kegan Paul, 1962), pp. 38–41.
18. I have discussed the Receptacle and the model Plato uses for it in more detail in chapter 2 of this book.
19. Joseph Stock, *Life of the Author*, included in *Works of George Berkeley*, ed. G. N. Wright, (London, 1843), p. x; originally published separately in 1776.

    One likely borrowing is Philonous' statement at *Dialogues*, I, sect. 10, "I am not for imposing any sense on your words: you are at liberty to explain them as you please. Only, I beseech you make me understand something by them." This echoes the remark of Socrates at *Charmides* 163, "I have no objection to your giving names any signification which you please, if you will only tell me what you mean by them." This parallel was first noticed by D. S. Robinson in his "The Platonic Model of *Hylas* and *Philonous*," *Philosophical Review* 29, 5 (1920): 484–87. Another parallel suggests that Berkeley was familiar with the *Timaeus* long before he became Junior Greek Lecturer at Trinity College in 1712. At *Principles*, sect. 32, Berkeley says that "the consistent uniform working" that we observe in nature "is so far from leading our thoughts to the First Cause that it rather sends them awandering after second causes." In the last phrase, Berkeley plays with two of Plato's titles for the same thing, "The Wandering Cause" *(he planomeni aitia)* of *Timaeus* 48A, and "Second Causes" *(sunaitias)* of *Timaeus* 46c.
20. Russell, *Problems of Philosophy*, p. 40.
21. The adjectives "complete" and "incomplete" are used, as we have seen, by more recent defenders of the traditional doctrine. See chapter 1 of this book.
22. In "Berkeley's Metaphysical Grammar," in *Berkeley: Principles, Text, and Critical Essays*, p. 34. See also Madhabendranath Mitra, *Language, Truth and Predication* (New Delhi: New Statesman Publishing Company, 1988), ch. 5.

23. Phillip Cummins explores this topic from a different approach in his "Hylas' Parity Argument," in *Berkeley: Critical and Interpretive Essays*, pp. 283–94.
24. See chapter 3 of this book.
25. "Arguments . . . Drawn Up in Geometrical Fashion," Definition IX.
26. See *Principles* 3 and 22. This view of the mind of Berkeley's God is presented also in a manuscript recently found by Bertil Belfrage at Columbia University among the Samuel Johnson papers. See Bertil Belfrage, "A Summary of Berkeley's Metaphysics in a Hitherto Unpublished Berkelian Manuscript" in *Berkeley Newsletter*, no. 3, 1979, pp. 1–4.

CHAPTER 5

1. See Colin Turbayne, in "Kant's Refutation of Dogmatic Idealism" in *Philosophical Quarterly*, V, 20 (July 1955) pp. 225–44, reprinted as "Kant's relation to Berkeley" in *Kant Studies Today*, Lewis White Beck, ed., Open Court Library of Philosophy, 1969, pp. 88–116, and in The Bobbs-Merrill Reprint Series in *Philosophy* (1969, *Philosophy*), 212. I try to show here that Kant was thoroughly familiar with and used Berkeley's writings. Perhaps Hamann had this view in mind when he wrote, "This much is certain: without Berkeley there would have been no Kant." Johann Georg Hamann, letter to Herder, April 20, 1782, in R. G. Smith, *Johann Georg Hamann, 1730–88* (New York: Harper, 1960).
2. Translations of the *Critique* are from *Immanuel Kant: Critique of Pure Reason*, Norman Kemp Smith, trans. (London: Macmillan, 1929). References to the first and second editions will be by page numbers and letters A and B respectively.
3. Gilbert Ryle, *Concept of Mind*, p. 168.
4. For additional detail, see chapter 3 of this text.
5. References in this chapter to Aristotle's works are to the *De Anima* unless otherwise stated.
6. See chapter 3. Kant's vocabulary is a mixture of the Procreation and Craftsmanship models.
7. Immanuel Kant, *Universal Natural History and Theory of the Heavens* (1755), translated from the German by W. Hastie in *Kant's Cosmogony* (Glasgow, 1900), pp. 135–36.
8. Isaac Newton, *Opticks* (1704), Query 28.
9. James Ward, *A Study of Kant* (Cambridge: University Press, 1922), pp. 60–61.
10. *Immanuel Kant: Prolegomena to Any Future Metaphysics*, with an introduction, ed. Lewis W. Beck, (New York: The Liberal Arts Press, 1950), p. 36.

CHAPTER 6

1. Paul Kolers, "Bilingualism and Information Processing," in *Scientific American* 218:3 (March 1968), pp. 78–86.
2. Plato's preoccupation with the letters of the alphabet is seen throughout his works. In the *Politicus* he presents the classical method of learning to read and then uses it as a model for learning "the long and difficult syllables of life" (278). Berkeley's interest in language combined with his interest in optics to produce his two works on vision: *An Essay towards a New Theory of Vision* and *The Theory of Vision or Visual Language Vindicated and Explained*. See C. M. Turbayne, ed., *George Berkeley: Works on Vision* (Westport, Conn.: Greenwood Press, 1981).
3. See *Myth of Metaphor*, ch. 5.
4. See Marius Von Senden, *Space and Sight* (Glencoe, Illinois: The Free Press, 1960; tr. Peter Heath, from German edn., 1932), pp. 106, 108, 114. The answers given here are to the problem of Molyneux: Can a man born blind and made to see, confronted for the first time with a cube and a sphere, tell by sight before he touches them which is the cube and which the sphere? Molyneux, an Irishman, sent the problem to Locke in 1692 who published it in his *Essay*. Both answered no. The problem became a central one in eighteenth-century philosophy and divided the empiricists from the nativists. Berkeley's philosophy, it seems likely to me, took its starting point from this celebrated problem. Von Senden presents sixty-six case histories and concludes: "The patient notices that these visual impressions awaken no familiar ideas in him, and that he cannot recognize the objects in question" (p. 299). A more recent case of a man "effectively blind since infancy" is presented by Richard Gregory in the *Times Literary Supplement*, 26 April 1974, p. 489, who reports that "we revealed a cube and a sphere to his newly opened eyes and asked him what he saw. He not only indicated that they differed; but named them correctly as square and round." This seems conclusive. In his earlier account of the same case, however, in his book *Recovery from Early Blindness* (Cambridge: Cambridge University Press, 1963). Gregory discloses that he did not examine his subject until forty-eight days after the operation (p. 16), and that the subject did not lose his sight until ten months after birth. Moreover, we learn that at his first visual experience when the bandages were removed after the operation, the patient "heard a voice coming from in front of him and to one side; he turned to the source of the sound, and saw a 'blur' " (p. 17). Von Senden says: "I am sure that this case does not alter the conclusions in my book" (*Recovery*, p. 46). These factors, I believe, vitiate Gregory's later account given above. For additional detail see *Myth of Metaphor*, pp. 109–12, and *Works on Vision*, n. 111.
5. *Space and Sight*, p. 108.

6. See John A. Downing, *The i.t.a. Reading Experiment* (London: University of London Institute of Education, 1964), pp. 5–25.
7. The artist, Vida Lahey, makes a plea for treating art as a language and asks: "Why should a child be trained in the composition of words but seldom in the composition of colors, forms, and sounds?" She continues: "Art, instead of being treated as a language the rudiments of which every child should practice and every youth should study in order to fit him to understand and enjoy the great heritage of artistic culture now available, is given comparatively small consideration, and by practical implication ranked as of minor importance in life." From "Art for All," lecture, 1940 in *The Art of Vida Lahey*, ed. Bettina MacAulay (Queensland Art Gallery, 1989), p. 88.
8. See ch. 2, p. 35, above for his other role as "the generative power in the world."
9. *Phaedrus* 275A.
10. *Theory of Vision*, 55. It seems likely to me that it was the rediscovery of glass and its use in windows in fifteenth-century Florence that triggered the discovery of perspective by Renaissance painters.
11. John Berger, *Success and Failure of Picasso* (Penguin, 1965), p. 160.
12. David Elkind, ed. *Six Psychological Studies* (New York: Random House, 1967), pp. 5, 14.

Name Index

Aesculapius, 27
Alexander of Aphrodisias, 43
Allaire, Edwin B., 69
Anaxagoras, 36–38
Anaximander, 84
Anaximenes, 84
Aphrodite, 32
Aquinas, St. Thomas, 43
Archimedes, 89
Aristarchus, 24, 89f.
Aristotle, 3, 5, 16, 17f. 21, 22, 30ff., 41–66, 67, 76–81, 84, 85, 87, 90ff., 117, 122, 125
Armstrong, D. M., 123
Athens, 23, 40f.
Ayer, A. J., 70, 123

Bacon, Francis, 14
Bacon, Roger, 53
Beck, Lewis White, 125
Belfrage, Bertil, 125
Berger, John, 113, 127
Berkeley, George, 5, 11, 65, 67–80, 82, 93f., 100, 111, 116–118, 119, 124, 126
Blanché, Robert, 124
Boswell, James, 119
Bracken, Harry M., 123
Bunyan, John, 3
Butler, Samuel, 110

Chalcidius, 27
Champollion, Jean Francois, 103
Cherniss, H. F., 120
Chiron, 27
Copernicus, Nicolaus, 86, 90, 94
Cornford, F. M., 23, 32, 120
Couvier, 42
Cummins, Phillip, 123, 125

Darwin, Charles, 42
Descartes, René, 1, 10, 20, 66, 67f., 79, 119
Doney, Willis, 123
Downing, John A., 127
Ducasse, C. J., 124
Dürer, Albrecht, 112

Einstein, Albert, 4, 24, 39, 121
Eliot, T. S., 121
Elkind, David, 127
Empedocles, 37
Euclid, 36f., 38, 117

Freud, Sigmund, 2

Gabo, Naum, 99f., 117
Galen, 53
Galileo, 24, 86
Grave, S. A., 70, 74, 123
Gregory, Richard, 126

Hamann, Johann Georg, 125
Hamlyn, D. W., 121
Harris, E. E., 124
Hastie, W., 125
Heath, Peter, 126
Herder, Johann Gottfried von, 125
Hermes, 35, 109
Hicks, R. D., 122
Hippocrates: on hysteria, 31
Hobbes, Thomas, 1f., 10f.
Hopper, Stanley Romaine, 120
Hume, David, 1f., 11–13, 14, 15, 67f., 70f., 77, 80, 119, 124

Ibn al Hatham (Alhazen), 53

Jesus, 65
Johnson, Dr. Samuel, 11, 119
Johnson, Samuel (President of King's College, New York), 125
Jones, W. H. S., 120

Kahn, Charles, 122
Kant, Immanuel, 1, 5, 67, 81, 82–94, 117, 125
Kemp Smith, Norman, 125
Kepler, Johannes, 24, 53, 86, 97f.
Klibansky, Raymond, 120
Kolers, Paul, 95, 126

Lady Macbeth, 30, 104
Lahey, Vida, 127
Linnaeus (Carl von Linné), 42

Locke, John, 126
Luce, A. A., 69

MacAulay, Bettina, 127
Macbeth, 96, 105
Marias, Julian, 24, 120
Marsh, R. C., 119
Martin, C. B., 123
Miller, David L., 120
Mitra, Madhabendranath, 124
Molyneux, William, 126
Moore, G. E., 51ff., 69, 71–73, 90, 122–24

Newman, James R., 121
Newton, Sir Isaac, 4, 24, 86, 125

Oaklander, L. N., 123
Onians, R. B., 120
Owen, G. E. L., 120

Pappas, George S., 123
Peck, A. L., 121
Piaget, Jean, 95, 118
Picasso, Pablo, 113
Pitcher, George, 70, 74, 123
Pitman, Sir James, 105f.
Plato, 3–5, 7ff., 15, 16f., 19, 21, 22–41, 42, 45, 51f., 59, 62, 64f., 67, 72, 74–76, 84f., 87, 89, 100, 109, 116, 124, 126
Plutarch, 89
Popper, Karl, 24
Preus, A., 121

Ramsey, F. P., 13–17, 19, 119
Randall, J. H., 121
Raphael, 27
Reid, Thomas, 7, 9, 13, 14, 15, 119
Robinson, D. S., 124
Ross, W. D., 60, 121, 122
Russell, Betrand, 9, 13f., 18f., 51ff., 71–73, 74, 77, 90, 119, 122, 124
Ryle, Gilbert, 1f., 74, 83, 119, 120, 124, 125

Schilpp, P. A., 124
Smith, R. G., 125
Socrates, 1, 65, 124
Steinkraus, Warren E., 123
Stock, Joseph, 76, 124
Strawson, P. F., 9, 13, 20, 119

Taylor, A. E., 23, 120
Theaetetus, 37
Themistius, 122
Thoth, 108f.
Turbayne, Colin M., 119, 123, 125, 156

Veith, Ilza, 121
Vlastos, Gregory, 120
Von Senden, Marius, 126

Ward, James, 88, 125
Watson, R., 123
Weyl, Herman, 37, 121
Wells, H. G., 101
Whitehead, A. N., 14
Wright, G. N., 124
Wrobel, J., 120

Zabarella, 60

Subject Index

Act and object, 50ff., 71f., 74, 90
Aether: the fifth substance, 31
Analysis and synthesis, 16f.
Aristotle's trinity, 48f., 56, 63f.
Art as a language, 127
Art, making works of, modeled upon writing, 108–16; photography, 110–12; painting, 111–13; sculpture, 113–16. See also Writing.
Atlantis, 23, 40f.

Basic triangles, 32, 34, 36f.; generate the regular solids, 37; and the testes, 38
Blind from birth, made to see, 102–6. See also Molyneux Problem; Vision: Visual illiteracy.
Byzantine tradition, 27

Camera, as model for vision, 97f., 106; and perspective, 111; photography distinguished from painting, 111–13
Cartesian-Newtonian tradition, 21
Category mistake, 119
Cause, efficient, 44f., 90f.; formal, 38, 40; material, 44; First, 124; Second, 40, 124; Wandering, 29, 124
Cogito ergo sum: argument for, 10
Collections of ideas, 72
Common sense (*sensus communis*), 56f.; and passive mind, 57, 59, 122
Common sensorium, 54f., 57, 63
Copernican Mind, 87–89
Copernican Revolution, Kant's, 84–86
Craftsman Model, 22, 27f., 29, 34, 38f., 44f., 65, 82, 87, 89, 120, 125

Definiendum-definiens theory, 77, 118
Demiurge, 27f., 32, 38f.
Diotima, 62
Distinction Principle, 67–74, 78–80
Divine seed, 31, 34

Embryo, 46, 76
Emission and Immission theories, 53
Energeia, 61, 72, 122
Energy, 39, 66
Eros, 30, 34, 121
Esse-percipi principle, 73

Faculty, 47; passive and active, 72, 74, 81, 83, 84, 85, 86
Father, 34, 39, 45; similar to the Good, 80, 94
Father image, 120
Female, 46; as material cause, 45
Forms, 34, 36, 38f., 87

God, 80, 86, 125
Good, the, 55; as Cause and Model Form, 40; similar to Father and Maker, 80, 94. See also Maker.

Hieroglyphs, 100–3, 110
Hysteria. See Wandering womb.

Ideal State, 24; actualized in ancient Athens, 40f.
Identity Principle, 67–74, 80
Illusion, 96–106
Imagination, 56ff., 72, 91; and images, 91f.
Immortality, 43, 48, 61f.
Inherence, 41, 67–69, 119
Inherence Principle, 67–69, 74, 76, 78–80
In the mind, 53f., 68, 76–80; and Plato's Receptacle, 54, 64, 74–76. See also Inherence Principle.
Intuition, 85, 90

Language, written and spoken, 100–8; ambiguity in, 96–106
"Large letters," 25, 41

Macrocosm, 26, 37, 90
Macropolis, 26
Maker: Cause of the cosmos, 28, 34; as craftsman, 28; as father, 28ff.; and phallus, 34; as Cause and Model Form, 40; cosmos as image of, 40; as maker of nature, 89. See also Good, the.
Male, 46; as efficient and formal cause, 45; as active, 45
Male and female, 34, 37, 39, 46, 47, 50, 52f., 59, 62; as efficient and material cause, 34, 45; and androgyny, 37
"Matter," from *meter* = mother, 22
Matter, 22, 32, 34, 40, 42, 44, 64, 66, 70, 77, 86; and menstrual fluid, 31

Subject Index

Menstrual fluid, 31, 46, 59; as prime matter, 34
Metaphor: defined, 3, 119; extended, 3f., 16, 24ff., two stages in life of, 3f.; root, 4; half-hidden, 23; Plato's definition of, 24; as pointed finger, 24f.; as large letters, 25; mixed, 39
Metaphorical Way, 3f., 44
Microcosm, 26, 37, 90
Micropolis, 26, 40
Mind: "the official theory" of, 1f.; substance-attribute theory of, 1ff., 6, 21, 41, 64, 66; active, 5, 60–63, 82, 91–94; as Reader and Writer, 6, 95; as substratum, 21, 63f., 66; passive and active, 21, 42f., 48f., 58, 71f., 80f., 82, 92f., 95; and *sensus communis*, 52; passive, 58ff., 62f., 80; thinking and objects of, 59; as spiritual substance, 63, 65, 74; phenomenalist account of, 70f., 78; Humean view of, 70f, 77f., androgynous, 80f.; Copernican Mind, 82; creative, 82, 93f.; and the sun, 94; and use of symbols, 95f.
Mind-centered universe, 94
Model: as extended metaphor, 3, 24ff.; defined, 16; modified, 18; used to test theory, 74–76
Model Form, 27ff., 40
Molyneux Problem, 126
Myth of the Earth-Born, 4, 7ff., 15, 19; and the class structure, 8f., 15

Necessity and Intelligence, 29, 32, 33, 41
Nurse, 29, 32, 34; wet, 31ff.; dry, 31ff. *See also* Receptacle.
Nutrition, 47f.

Offspring, 63f.

Particular, 13, 17f.; defined, 17f.; atomic, 79
Perception, 48ff., 85, 116; direct and indirect objects of, 48f.; emission and immission theories of, 53; proper and incidental objects of, 54; causal theory of, 49f., 90; modeled by reading, 116
Perspective, 111f.; defined, 111; discovery of triggered by rediscovery of glass, 127
Phallus, 30f., 34ff., 41, 46; models the Maker, 34; symbolizes generative power of cosmos, 34f.
philia: cement of the universe, 35
Plato's Receptacle. *See* Receptacle.

Plato's "secret doctrine," 51f.
Plato's trinity, 40f.
Pneuma (spirit), 32, 36, 38f., 46, 56, 58, 62, 65. *See also* semen.
Predication, 67–69, 119
Preformation: versus epigenesis, 38f.
Primary and secondary qualities, 55
Procreation Model, 5f., 22, 28–38, 45–47, 55, 58, 64–66, 67, 80, 82, 94f., 117, 125
Ptolemaic mind, 85–87

Reading: vision modeled upon, 100–8; two languages involved in, 100–8; defined, 102f.; and illiteracy, 102ff.; initial teaching alphabet for, 106; perceiving modeled upon, 116–18
Receptacle, 29f., 32, 34, 39, 40f., 45, 46, 54, 74–76, 80, 87, 124; as mother, 30; as space, 36, 86; as space and matter, 40; as model for mind, 64, 80; and sensibility, 87; as womb, 94. *See also* Nurse, womb.
Regular solids, 37
Root metaphor, 4, 23, 39
Rosetta stone, 100, 108

Semen, 30f., 36, 41, 46; models the Forms, 34. *See also pneuma*.
Sense data, 51
Sensibility, as passive faculty, 83–85, 88, 89, 91f.; as receptacle, 87
Sexual intercourse, 30–32, 34, 40f., 46, 63f., 113; models union of passive and active minds, 63f., 66; of Will and Understanding, 72, 92; of sense organ and external object, 72, 84; models interaction of energy and matter, 39
Signs, 100; artifical and natural, 95
Son of Cleon, 122
Son of Diares, 49f., 122
Soul, 44, 64f., 66; as efficient cause, 44; not a subject or substratum, 65; as lifeforce, 65. *See also pneuma* (spirit).
Space, 32, 36, 40. *See also* Receptacle.
Spirit. *See pneuma*.
Subject-predicate and substance-attribute parallel, 4, 7, 9, 13, 18, 20f., 77, 82, 118
Subject-predicate distinction, 4, 7, 9ff., 13, 17f., 65, 76–80; as model, 16, 19, 21; subject defined, 17f.; its basis, 13, 66

Subject Index

Subject-predicate model. *See* substance-attribute model.
Subject, predicated of a, 64, 69, 76–80; in a, 53, 54, 64, 76–80, 90, 93; completeness of, 13, 21, 27, 24
Substance, 67f; as substratum, 63, 65, 94; as essence, 63, 65; spiritual, 65; material, 80
Substance-attribute dichotomy, 4, 6, 10–13, 15, 66f., 69; and subject-predicate distinction, 4, 7, 9ff., 13ff., 15–17; its basis, 13, 66; meaning of substance, 17f.; as model, 19, 21
Substance-attribute model, 22, 42, 64, 95, 118
Symbols, 95f.

Understanding, 5, 21, 41, 80, 91f.; and Plato's Receptacle, 5, 93; as passive faculty, 72, 80; as active faculty, 83, 89; as craftsman, 88; as efficient cause, 88; as faculty of rules, 89; as Lawgiver of Nature; 89
Universal, 13, 17f.; defined, 17

Vision, Copy or Representative theory of, 97, 100, 103; Camera model for, 97f., 106; Language model for, 100–8; visual illiteracy, 103ff. *See also* Reading.

Wandering Cause, 29, 33. *See also* Cause.
Wandering womb, 30, 34
Will, 5, 41, 56f., 80; as active power, 72, 74, 80, 92; God's and mine, 72, 74
Wizard of Oz, 4, 113
Womb, 30, 38, 41, 94; in which, 31, 32, 46f., 56, 76; out of which, 31, 34, 46
Writing, models making works of art, 108–16; defined, 109; Seated Scribe as symbol for, 109f.